FIRSTS, LASTS
& ONLYS
GOLF

FIRSTS, LASTS
& ONLYS

PAUL DONNELLEY

PRESENTS THE MOST AMAZING

GOLF

FACTS FROM THE LAST 600 YEARS

HAMLYN

DEDICATION

In loving memory of Jeremy Beadle, MBE (1948–2008): mentor, counsellor, curator of oddities, and always a friend in need.

An Hachette UK Company
www.hachette.co.uk

First published in Great Britain in 2010 by
Hamlyn, a division of Octopus Publishing Group Ltd
Endeavour House
189 Shaftesbury Avenue
London
WC2H 8JY
www.octopusbooks.co.uk

ISBN 978-0-600-62174-4

A CIP catalogue record for this book is available from the British
Library

Printed and bound in China

10 9 8 7 6 5 4 3 2 1

THE FIRSTS

THE FIRST

THE FIRST (cont.)

THE FIRST (cont.)

THE FIRST (cont.)

THE FIRST (cont.)

THE FIRST (cont.)

THE FIRST (cont.)

THE LASTS

THE LAST

THE LAST (cont.)

THE ONLYS

THE ONLY

THE ONLY (cont.)

THE ONLY (cont.)

THE ONLY (cont.)

INTRODUCTION

Golf is a game that is played in virtually every country of the world. It has a long and venerable history going back 700 or so years. As such, this book could not hope to be a comprehensive history of the game; it does, however, take a lively look at some of the more interesting aspects of golf over the years. Hopefully, it will find favour with fans young and old as they dip into stories about golf and its players past and present.

One wag described golf as 'an infuriating game that brings out the worst in people. Why was it called golf? Because all the other four letter words were taken.' Another rather sexist player suggested that golf stood for 'Gentleman Only, Ladies Forbidden' – tell that to Babe Zaharias or, more recently, Michelle Wie! Mark Twain called golf 'a good walk spoiled' but how wrong was he! The terrific thing about what Nick Faldo calls 'this great game' is that it can be played and enjoyed by all ages, virtually all fitness levels, and yes, of course, by men and women.

John Updike said, 'Golf appeals to the idiot in us and the child. Just how childlike golf players become is proven by their frequent inability to count up to five.' Britain's wartime prime minister, Sir Winston Churchill, said, 'Golf is a game whose aim is to hit a very small ball into an even smaller hole, with weapons singularly ill-designed for the purpose.' The creator of *Winnie the Pooh*, A. A. Milne opined, 'Golf is popular because it is the best game in the world at which to be bad.'

The game also gives you an excuse to wear loud clothes in public without being the subject of derision, well ... not too much. Tiger Woods said, '[Ice] Hockey is a sport for white men. Basketball is a sport for black men. Golf is a game for white men dressed as black pimps.'

Where possible I have included the locations and full dates for events. This has proved to be more difficult than I first imagined because although golfing legend is littered with incredible stories and who won what, it is poorly served when it comes to when. Unlike football and especially cricket, most golf sources and reference books list only the year of an event rather than the day and month. It is relatively easy to find the exact date of the 1873 FA Cup Final or the Eton-Harrow cricket match in 1815, but it is much more difficult trying to ascertain the exact date of the 1903 Open. Therefore, I hope readers will indulge me if an entry is not totally complete as to who won what and when.

The book can be read in one sitting, dipped into at will or even used as a quiz book at the 19th hole. If that idea takes your fancy, perhaps you could begin with the following 'teesers':

* *How did an archbishop's innocent interest in golf lead to the 16-year long Rabbit Wars?*
* *Who was the first woman to play in a man's tournament and why did she have to?*
* *Which tournament winner gets to hold a trophy designed by Rodman Wanamaker?*
* *Who was the champion described as having 'the face of an angel and the temper of a timber wolf'?*
* *Which club apologized for any inconvenience that might be caused by the lady competitors of the Curtis Cup Match entering the clubhouse?*
* *How did one man idly fondling a piece of rubber change the course of golf?*
* *Which US Open golf champion found solace in the arms of another woman after his wife lost interest in him and his career?*
* *How did two American dentists revolutionize the tee-thing industry?*
* *How did Jerry Pate celebrate winning a tournament in 1981?*
* *Who is the only player to appear on banknotes?*
* *How did the wind cost Tommy Bolt $250?*
* *Which world leader managed a score of 34 - 38 under par on his very first round of golf?*

AUTHOR ACKNOWLEDGEMENTS

This book could not have been written without the inspiration of Jeremy Beadle, MBE. He was a most brilliant oddity hunter – the broadcaster Michael Aspel labelled him 'the nation's curator of oddities' – a generous mentor and a warm-hearted man.

I would also like to thank the following for help, inspiration and kindness: Mindy Bianca, Hershey Entertainment & Resorts PR director; Ian Bunch, secretary of the Prestwick Golf Club; Trevor Davies at Hamlyn; John Duncan, secretary-manager of Royal Dornoch Golf Club; my agent Chelsey Fox; Gavin Fuller of the Telegraph Media Group; Ian Harrison; Kay Maghan, Hershey Entertainment & Resort assistant PR director; Scott Henderson, general manager and chief operating officer of the Royal Mayfair Golf Club; Donald McDonald, secretary of the Royal Perth Golfing Society; Trevor Montague; Jennifer Morton, Museum and Heritage Assistant Curator of the Royal & Ancient Club; Glenda Mulder, Laurens Public Library, Laurens, Iowa; Office of History and Preservation, Office of the Clerk, US House of Representatives; Mitchell Symons; Mike Thomas, finance convenor at Royal Dornoch Golf Club; Heidi Wegmueller of the Professional Golfers' Association; Pamela C. Whitenack, Hershey Community Archives director; and my wonderful and patient wife Karima, who makes all things in my life not only possible but enjoyable.

Paul Donnelley
Oran, Algeria and Essex, England, 2010
www.pauldonnelley.com

ABBREVIATIONS AND GLOSSARY

Ace - A hole in one.

Air shot - A swing that misses the ball but still counts as a stroke on the scorecard.

Albatross - A hole completed in three under par (also known as a double eagle).

Back nine - The second set of holes on a golf course (10–18).

Bantam Ben - Nickname for Ben Hogan.

Beach - A sand bunker.

Big Easy - Nickname for Ernie Els.

Birdie - A hole completed in one under par.

Black Knight - Nickname for Gary Player.

Bogey - One over the par score for the hole.

Buzzard - Two over the par score for the hole.

Choke - To lose a match that was seemingly already won.

Cup - The hole on the green into which the ball must be put.

Cut - Divide in a competition where some competitors are allowed to continue and some leave.

Eagle - A hole completed in two under par.

Fore! - Shouted warning to other golfers and spectators that a ball is on the way. *The Shorter Oxford English Dictionary* recorded the first usage in 1878 but no one has been able to suggest a definitive etymology of the word.

Foozle - To mess up a stroke.

Four-ball - A match in which two players (side) play their better ball against the better ball of the two other players (side).

Foursome - A match where two players compete against two other players in alternate-shot format, with each side playing just one ball.

Frog hair - Short grass on the edge of a green.

Front nine - The first set of holes on a golf course (1–9).

Golden Bear - Nickname for Jack Nicklaus.

Great White Shark - Nickname for Greg Norman

Green jacket - The winner of the US Masters is presented with a green jacket. They are allowed to keep the garment for a year and then must return it to Augusta where it is kept for them. One player refused to return his green jacket.

Guttie - A type of golf ball (obsolete) (see 1848, page 38).

Jigger - Four-iron.

Jungle - Heavy overgrowth.

King, The - Nickname for Arnold Palmer.

Kitty litter - Another name for a sand bunker.

Links - A golf course four miles or less from the seaside.

LPGA - Ladies Professional Golfers' Association

Matchplay - Scoring system in which a player, or team, earns a point for each hole in which they have beaten an opponent.

Nineteenth hole - The clubhouse bar.

Par - A term originated at the London Stock Exchange where a stock price was equal to the face value of the stock. In 1911 the USPGA issued measurements for determining par scores that are still in use today. A hole up to 225 yards long is par 3, 226 yards to 425 yards is par 4, 426 yards to 600 yards is par 5 and more than 600 yards is par 6.

PGA - Professional Golfers' Association.

Pin - Pole in the hole or cup on the green, topped with a flag.

Quad - A hole completed in four over par, or a quadruple bogey.

Sclaff - To hit the ground before you hit the ball in a swing.

Scratch - Par score for the hole.

Silver Scot, The - Nickname for Tommy Armour.

Singles - A match in which one player plays against another.

Squire, The - Nickname for Gene Sarazen.

Stroke play - A scoring system in which the total number of strokes over one or more rounds of 18 holes is counted.

Stymie - A law abolished in 1952 which stated that if a ball was in line of the hole (unless the distance was six inches or fewer) you would have to chip over it or play around it.

Trap - Americanism for a bunker.

USGA - United States Golf Association.

USPGA- United States Professional Golfers' Association.

WAG - Wife and/or girlfriend of a player.

Yips - An uncontrollable shaking in the hands and arms before an important putt.

THE FIRST
ILLUSTRATION OF GOLF

GLOUCESTER CATHEDRAL, 12 COLLEGE GREEN,
GLOUCESTER, GLOUCESTERSHIRE, ENGLAND.
1340-1350

There is a stained glass window at Gloucester Cathedral showing a headless man on a green background swinging a club at a yellow ball. The window, which is in the eastern façade, was commissioned by Sir Thomas Broadstone in commemoration of his friends and comrades who died at the Battle of Crécy south of Calais in northern France (26 August 1346) in the Hundred Years War. Edward III of England (1312–1377) commanded around 12,000 troops against Philip VI (1293–1350) of France's force of 35,000 but was victorious thanks in no small part to the superiority of the English longbowmen. English casualties were light but thousands of Frenchmen and their allies were killed.

THE FIRST
REFERENCE TO A SPORT
SIMILAR TO GOLF

Flanders, Belgium. 1353 or 1354

In Flanders in 1353 or 1354 a reference was made to 'chole', a then-popular game played in fields. The game was played by two individuals or teams and the first had to hit a ball with a club and aim for a specific target. The second's job was, on every fourth go, to hit the ball into a hazard such as thick grass, a pond or some such obstacle.

THE FIRST
REFERENCE TO SCOTTISH
PLAYERS OF 'CHOLE'

Siege of Baugé, France. 21 March 1421

At the Siege of Baugé the Scots helped the French fight against the English (not for the first or last time – the French-Scots alliance is known as the 'Auld Alliance' and persisted for several centuries). The French introduced their Tartan allies to the game of chole. The Scots were much taken with the game and Hugh Kennedy, Robert Stewart and John Smale are said to have introduced the game to Scotland. The broadcaster Alistair Cooke opined that, 'Golf was just what the Scottish character had been seeking for centuries, a method of self-torture disguised as a game.'

THE FIRST
RECORDED
BANNING
OF GOLF

SCOTLAND. MARCH 1457

The Scottish Parliament of James II (1437–1460) issued a decree in March 1457 banning golf because it interfered with men practising archery, a much-needed skill in the wars against England. The law stated that 'goff be utterly cryit doune and not usit'. Football was also proscribed for the same reason although that ban dated back to 1424. When James III (1451–1488) ascended to the throne, he, too, banned golf in 1470, as did James IV (1488–1513) in 1491. It was not until the signing of the Treaty of Glasgow in 1502 that the ban was lifted.

THE FIRST
RECORDED PURCHASE
OF GOLF EQUIPMENT
PERTH, SCOTLAND. WEDNESDAY 21 SEPTEMBER 1502

James IV of Scotland, the grandson of James II, made the first recorded purchase of golf equipment when he bought a set of golf clubs and balls from a bow-maker in Perth in the autumn of 1502. Unsurprisingly, the clubs were very different from today's sleek objects of desire. Players would use clubs called 'longnoses' for driving, grassed drivers for medium shots, 'spoons' for short shots, niblicks and a cleek for putting. The shafts were made of hazel or ash wood, while the head would be manufactured from beech or a similar material. The shaft was tightly bound in leather but this was still not sufficiently strong and many players broke clubs during rounds.

In 1826 club-maker Robert Forgan of Fife began using hickory wood for the shafts but as it made clubs expensive to produce, some club-makers continued to utilise other woods. In the 1920s steel shafts began to replace wooden ones and steel was later replaced by graphite.

THE FIRST
RECORDED NON-ROYAL GOLFER
SIR ROBERT MAULE AT BARRY LINKS, ANGUS, SCOTLAND. 1527

Sir Robert Maule (1497–1560) was the first non-royal golfer recorded in history. He is said to have played a round on Barry Links, Angus, which is near the modern-day town of Carnoustie. Sir Robert was described by contemporaries as:

'ane man of comlie behaviour, of hie stature, sanguine in collure both of hyd and haire, colarique of nature and subject to suddane anger ... He had gryt delight in haukine and hountine ... Lykewakes he exercisit the gowf, and ofttimes past to Barry Links, quhan the wadsie was for drink.'

The 'wadsie' was a wager or bet.

THE FIRST
RECORDED GAME AT
ST ANDREWS
St Andrews, Fife, Scotland. 1552

In the place generally regarded as the home of golf, the first recorded game of golf took place in 1552. Oddly, seven holes at the Old Course at St Andrews share two holes each – the only 'exclusive' holes are the first, ninth, 17th and 18th. In addition, the course can be played clockwise or anti-clockwise.

THE FIRST
ECCLESIASTICAL DECREE
ALLOWING GOLF
ST ANDREWS, FIFE, SCOTLAND. 1553

A year after the game was first played at St Andrews, John Hamilton (1511–1571), the Archbishop of St Andrews, issued an ecclesiastical decree that gave the local people the right to play golf on the links at St Andrews. John Hamilton had become archbishop in 1546 but was imprisoned in 1563 having fallen foul of Protestants. When he was released the archbishop became an active supporter of Mary, Queen of Scots (1542–1587) and baptised her son, the future James I and VI (1566–1625). His nephew, James Hamilton, assassinated James Stuart, Earl of Murray, the Regent of Scotland in 1570. The archbishop was arrested and charged with complicity in the murders of Murray and Henry Stuart, Lord Darnley (see below). He was hanged on 6 April 1571. In 1611 Archbishop George Gledstanes confirmed Archbishop Hamilton's decree regarding golf and in 1620 James VI granted a charter ratifying Gledstanes's and Hamilton's decree.

THE FIRST

RECORDED
FEMALE GOLFER

**Mary, Queen of Scots at Seton Palace, East Lothian, Scotland.
February 1567**

The cousin of Elizabeth I, Mary was a devout Roman Catholic and the bane of Elizabeth's life. Mary ascended to the throne when she was just six days old, on the death of her father James V. On 29 July 1565 at Holyrood Palace Mary married Henry Stuart, Lord Darnley, her Roman Catholic half first cousin. The marriage angered Elizabeth who had suggested one of her favourites, Robert Dudley, 1st Earl of Leicester, as a potential groom, but Mary loved Darnley.

He was a brutal man and on 9 March 1566, when Mary was six months' pregnant, murdered her secretary David Rizzio in front of her. Their son, the future King James I of England and Scotland was born on 19 June 1566. At the end of the year Darnley became ill with either smallpox or, according to some sources, syphilis. On 1 February 1567 Darnley moved to Kirk o' Fields, a pleasant house some 10 minutes' walk from Holyrood Palace in Edinburgh, to recuperate. Darnley was to return to Holyrood on 10 February. At 2 am on that day the house was destroyed in an explosion of a dozen barrels of gunpowder three hours after Mary had left to attend the marriage of her favourite valet Bastian Pages to one of her favourite gentlewomen Christina Hogg.

The partially clad bodies of Darnley and his valet William Taylor were found in the garden, the cause of death, strangulation. The explosion had either been an attempt to cover up the murders or Darnley had somehow learned of the plot, tried to escape but was caught in the garden and throttled.

Not long after Darnley's death, Mary was seen playing golf at Sefton House and was criticised by the Calvinist John Knox (1514–1572) and the church for such callousness. Mary had young pages carry her bags and called them cadets, which may be where the word 'caddie' comes from.

THE FIRST

REFERENCE TO GOLF

IN THE WEST OF SCOTLAND

GLASGOW, SCOTLAND. 1589

The game was banned in the Blackfriars Yard, Glasgow. This is the first reference to golf in the west of Scotland. It would be more than 100 years later – in 1721 – that the earliest reference would be made to golf at Glasgow Green, the first course in the west of Scotland.

THE FIRST

REFERENCE TO BANNING GOLF
ON THE SABBATH

Edinburgh, Scotland. 1592

Three years after the first reference to golf in Glasgow, the Royal Burgh of Edinburgh banned golfing at Leith on Sunday 'in tyme of sermonis'. Nine years earlier, two St Andrews boys had been rebuked by Kirk Session for golfing on the Sabbath.

THE FIRST

REFERENCE TO THE FEATHERIE BALL

MONOPOLY GRANTED TO JAMES MELVILL. 1618

Prior to the invention of the featherie ball, it is thought that balls were made of turned boxwood, similar to those used in 'chole' and pall mall. At the time a monopoly was granted to James Melvill – he sold each featherie ball for 4d.

The featherie was made from goose or chicken feathers and painted. There were enough feathers in the ball to fill a top hat – roughly half a gallon. They were boiled and put into a bag made of wet horse- or cowhide. As the hide shrank, the feathers expanded to make a tight ball. It was then covered in paint. If the hide split, then it would be stitched shut. The problem with the featherie was that in wet weather the stitching would rot and if the ball hit a hard object such as a rock, it could split open.

The longest drive recorded with a featherie was 361 yards (330 metres). Another problem was the expense – some featheries were more expensive to buy than clubs as the top makers could only make three or four each day. Other notable ball-makers of the 1600s were Andrew Dickson of Leith and Henry Mills of St Andrews. It might be worth your while keeping an eye open at car boot sales or searching the attic of an ageing relative – featheries have been sold at auction for more than £13,000 ($20,000).

THE FIRST
REFERENCE TO CADDIES
MONTROSE, SCOTLAND. 1628

The Marquis of Montrose was a keen golfer as was his father, the earl. In their accounts are references to their golf expenses including in 1628 the payment of four shillings 'to the boy who carried my clubs'. The first named caddie was Andrew Dickson, who worked as a caddie for the Duke of York in 1682 in the first international match (see 1682, page 29); there is also some evidence that Mary, Queen of Scots may have called the pages who carried her clubs 'cadets' from which the word caddie is derived (see 1567, page 25)

THE FIRST

DEATH
AS A RESULT OF GOLF
Kelso, Scotland. 1632

In 1632 Thomas Clatto was watching a golf match in a churchyard in Kelso when he was struck under the left ear by a ball. He died later, apparently as a result of the blow.

THE FIRST

REBELLION DURING A GAME
LEITH, SCOTLAND. OCTOBER 1641

Charles I (1600–1649), king of England, Scotland and Ireland, was playing golf at Leith when word was brought to him of the Irish rebellion, marking the beginning of the English Civil War (1641–1651). He finished his round, but eventually lost his head.

THE FIRST

REFERENCE TO GOLF
IN LONDON
Westminster, London. 1658

Golf was first mentioned as being played in London at 'Up Fields', now Vincent Square, in Westminster, London. The square is owned by Westminster School and it has served as playing fields for its pupils for several centuries.

THE FIRST
REFERENCE TO GOLF IN AMERICA
ALBANY, NEW YORK, AMERICA. 1659

The first reference to golf in America is also the first reference to banning the game on the streets of Albany, New York. It would be almost 70 years before the first golf club was founded in America but the game was certainly played by individuals. When the governor of New York and Massachusetts William Bennett died in 1729 'nine clubs, one iron ditto and seven dozen balls' were among his possessions.

THE FIRST
RECORDED INTERNATIONAL MATCH
SCOTLAND VS ENGLAND AT LEITH, EDINBURGH, SCOTLAND. 1682

The first recorded match between two competing nations saw James, Duke of York and John Paterson (in some references Paterstone), a shoemaker, playing for Scotland against two peers who wore England's favours. Scotland won the match.

THE FIRST
BOOK ON GOLF CLUB MANUFACTURE
United Kingdom. 1687

In 1687 Thomas Kincaid, a medical student in Edinburgh, wrote *Thoughts on Golve*, in diary form, the first book to feature information on how golf clubs were made.

THE FIRST
MATCH REPORTED IN A
NEWSPAPER

LEITH, EDINBURGH, SCOTLAND. 1724

The first recorded large bet was for 20 guineas and was contested in 'a solemn match of golf' by Alexander Elphinstone, a younger son of Lord Balmerino, and Captain John Porteous of the Edinburgh City Guard. Oddly, there is no record of who actually won the bet. Five years later at the same venue, Elphinstone fought and won a duel.

Captain Porteous would lend his name to the Porteous Riots of 1736, when he shot into a crowd at the execution of Andrew Wilson, a merchant and local favourite. Following Porteous's trial and acquital he was lynched by an angry mob.

THE FIRST
NOVEL ABOUT GOLF
THE GOFF. 1743

In 1743 Thomas Mathison wrote an epic verse novel, the first about the game. The book was published in Edinburgh under the title *The Goff* and was an extended poem in 358 lines of three cantos, and is a picaresque description of a match between two golfers played at the five-hole links at Leith. It had two subsequent editions and all copies are very rare.

Mathison was a law clerk who was diverted by golf, poetry and the Presbyterian ministry; he died in 1754.

THE FIRST

RECORDED GOLF CLUB

Leith, Edinburgh, Scotland. March 1744

The first recorded golf club was the Gentlemen Golfers (now the Honourable Company of Edinburgh Golfers), which was formally constituted in the Scottish capital. The players competed for a silver trophy that was given to them by the City of Edinburgh. An open championship at Leith would decide who won the cup. Twenty years later, participation was restricted to members of the Honourable Company of Edinburgh Golfers.

THE FIRST

GOLF RULES

LEITH, EDINBURGH, SCOTLAND. WEDNESDAY 7 MARCH 1744

The game's first rules were drawn up on 7 March 1744. Ten years later, on 14 May 1754, the first codified Rules of Golf were published by the St Andrews Golfers (later the Royal & Ancient Golf Club of St Andrews) at their foundation by 22 noblemen and gentlemen of Fife. The first Rules of Golf drafted by Duncan Forbes contained just 13 laws. The latest (2010–2011) *Decisions on The Rules of Golf* contains 719 pages with an index listing more than 5,000 entries. All the world's participants in the game excluding the United States of America and Mexico would adhere to the rules.

In 1754 the St Andrews golfers also bought a silver cup to be played for on the Old Course. Bailie William Landale, a merchant of St Andrews, was the first champion beating off the challenge of 22 noblemen and others of Fife. The winner of the cup became club captain for a year. In 1806 the club began a gold medal competition and in 1834 William IV (1765–1837) became the club's patron.

BETTER NEVER THAN LATE

In 1939 the number of clubs permissible in a bag was limited to 14, to prevent players gaining an unfair advantage. In July 2001 Ian Woosnam was penalized two strokes at The Open at Lytham St Annes for having 15 clubs in his bag – an extra driver. His caddie Miles Byrne had failed to count the number in the bag at the first tee of the final round. Woosnam yelled at Byrne, 'I give you one job to do and you can't even get that right!' A fortnight later, Woosnam sacked Byrne after he was late for the start of the Scandinavian Masters at Malmo, Sweden. Woosnam had had to find a replacement caddie and break into his own locker to get his golf shoes.

In 1910 the Royal & Ancient banned the centre-shafted putter but in the United States it was still legal according to the US Golf Association, which began a 42-year period with two official but different versions of The Rules of Golf. In 1919 the Royal & Ancient took control of The Open Championship and The Amateur Championship. In 1951 the Royal & Ancient held a conference with the US Golf Association and several conflicts were resolved but not the issue over the size of the ball – the Royal & Ancient decreed it to be 1.62 inches (41.1 mm) and the US Golf Association 1.68 inches (42.6 mm). The centre-shafted putter was legalized worldwide and the out-of-bounds penalty standardized at stroke-and-distance while the stymie was finally abolished. In 1987 the Royal & Ancient adopted the 1.68 inch (42.6 mm) diameter ball, 38 years after it refused to sanction it. This was the first time since 1910 that The Rules of Golf were standardized throughout the world.

FIRST

GOLF TOURNAMENT

LEITH, EDINBURGH, SCOTLAND. MONDAY 2 APRIL 1744

The first recorded golf tournament – for the silver cup presented to the Gentlemen Golfers by the City of Edinburgh – was won by John Rattray.

THE FIRST
RECORDED GOLF CLUB
OUTSIDE SCOTLAND
London, England. 1745

The Blackheath Club was formed in southeast London by a group of noblemen who laid out a seven-hole course, the first recorded club south of the border. A silver driver was donated to the club as a prize. It became a 'Royal' club in 1857.

THE FIRST
MENTION OF
STROKEPLAY
ST ANDREWS, FIFE, SCOTLAND. 1759

Up until this time, all golf had consisted of matches. In 1764 the first four holes at St Andrews were combined into two, reducing the round from 22 holes (11 out and in) to 18 (nine out and in). Thus St Andrews became the first 18-hole golf course, which became the standard for all future courses.

THE FIRST
GOLF CLUB HOUSE
LEITH, EDINBURGH, SCOTLAND. 1768

Now an integral part of every golf course, the first club house was erected at Leith. It was called the Golf House; before that players used the local pub to change or discuss their strokes.

THE FIRST

PART-TIME
GOLF PROFESSIONAL
EDINBURGH, SCOTLAND. 1774

The Edinburgh Burgess Golfing Society was formed in 1773 and the following year they hired the first part-time golf course professional. He was also responsible for keeping the greens neat, tidy and playable. Most early golf professionals also made golf balls and/or worked as caddies.

THE FIRST

RECORDED GOLF CLUB
OUTSIDE THE
UNITED KINGDOM
THE SOUTH CAROLINA GOLF CLUB, CHARLESTON,
SOUTH CAROLINA, USA. 1786

The South Carolina Golf Club was founded in Charleston, the first recorded outside of the United Kingdom. In the same year the Crail Golfing Society was formed but neither have any continuity to the present day. The oldest club still operating in North America is the Montreal Golf Club, which was founded on 4 November 1873. It is believed that the fur traders of the Hudson Bay Company may have played golf before the establishment of the first recorded club in North America, the Montreal Golf Club. The club became the Royal Montreal in 1884. Twelve years later, the Royal Canadian Golfing Association became the sport's governing body.

THE FIRST

RABBIT WARS

St Andrews, Fife, Scotland. 1805

In 1552 Archbishop Hamilton had been granted permission to establish a rabbit warren on the links of St Andrews. In 1726 William Gib was also allowed to put rabbits on the links as long as they did not harm the golfing areas. In 1799 rabbits were introduced on a commercial scale by Charles and Cathcart Dempster who had bought rights to the links. Two years later, George Cheape, the captain of the Society of St Andrews Golfers, made an official complaint that the rabbits were wrecking the links. It took a further four years of destruction before the Court of Session gave the local people the right to kill rabbits on the links, which gave rise to the nickname of 'the Rabbit Wars'. The Wars continued until 1821 when James Cheape of Strathtyrum bought the links.

THE FIRST

WOMEN'S GOLF GOLF TOURNAMENT

MUSSELBURGH LINKS, THE OLD GOLF COURSE, BALCARRES ROAD, MUSSELBURGH, EAST LOTHIAN, SCOTLAND. WEDNESDAY 9 JANUARY 1811

The first golf tournament for women was organized by the Musselburgh Golf Club for the town's fishwives. The prizes were a creel and shawl, and two Barcelona handkerchiefs.

THE FIRST
INTER-CLUB
GOLF MATCH
BRUNTSFIELD, EDINBURGH, SCOTLAND. THURSDAY 4 JUNE 1818

The first inter-club golf match was a competition between Edinburgh Burgess Golfing Society and Bruntsfield Links Golf Club.

THE FIRST
HOLE-CUTTING
MACHINE
Musselburgh Links, The Old Golf Course, Balcarres Road, Musselburgh, East Lothian, Scotland. 1829

In 1829 the first hole-cutting machine was introduced at Musselburgh and it produced holes or cups that measured $4\frac{1}{4}$ inches (107.9 mm) in diameter. In 1893 The Royal & Ancient Golf Club of St Andrews decreed that holes should be the same size the world over and decided that the size should be the one in use at Musselburgh.

THE FIRST
RECORDED GOLF CLUB
IN INDIA
THE DUM DUM GOLFING CLUB AT DUM DUM, CALCUTTA, INDIA. 1829

The first recorded golf club in India was, not surprisingly, founded by members of the British Raj. The club was founded on what is today the site of Calcutta's international airport. After several moves it settled in 1910 in the city's southern suburbs on what is now 18 Golf Club Road. Originally, it had 36 holes but had to sell the land on which 18 of the holes were situated, in order to keep up with the costs.

The Dum Dum changed its name to the Calcutta Golf Club and later became the Royal Calcutta Club, the first on the sub-continent. The All-India Amateur Golf Championship was first held here in 1892 and remained till 1958, when it was played at the Delhi Golf Course for the first time, after it was decided to rotate the tournament between Delhi, Bombay and Calcutta.

THE FIRST

GOLF CLUB
WITH ROYAL TITLE

Royal Perth Golfing Society, Princes Street, Perth, Scotland. Tuesday 4 June 1833

The Perth Golfing Society was founded by a small number of gentlemen from Perth on 5 April 1824 at a meeting in the Salutation Inn, Scotland's oldest hotel. Players were obliged to wear scarlet golfing jackets for matches on the South Inch and North Inch links and Sir David Moncreiffe was the first captain. The first club headquarters was a room rented for £5 a year in Princes Street, Perth, where members could keep their golf clubs.

In 1833, thanks to the royal connections of the club's sixth captain, Lord Kinnaird, William IV conferred the distinction of 'Royal' on the club, making it the Royal Perth, beating The Royal & Ancient Golf Club of St Andrews by a year. In 1836 premises at 3 Charlotte Street, Perth were purchased for £150 and fitted out for an additional £70. In 1875 the club bought its present premises at 1 Atholl Crescent, Perth. In 1878, the club name was expanded to become The Royal Perth Golfing Society and County and City Club.

THE FIRST
GUTTA-PERCHA
GOLF BALL

INVENTED BY EDINBURGH UNIVERSITY STUDENT IN 1848

The first gutta-percha ball was invented by Scottish-born Rev. Dr Robert Adams Patterson in 1848. A keen golfer as a student at Edinburgh University, Patterson had been too poor to buy pigskin balls so he experimented with other materials. His most successful had been the gutta-percha, wrapped around an idol sent to him from India. The dried sap of a sapodilla tree was used to make the gutta or guttie. The sap was rubber-like in consistency and could be moulded while hot.

Cheaper than the featherie, it also had the advantage of flying further. Unfortunately, the gutta-percha proved difficult for golfers to hit out of both fairways and the rough. In 1881 dimples began appearing on gutta-percha balls after players noticed that the ball flew much better once it had been scuffed. It would not be until 1905 that William Taylor in England patented the first dimple-pattern for golf balls. It might be worth searching an attic or keeping an eye open at car boot sales – a gutta-percha in good condition can be worth as much as £330 ($500).

THE FIRST
GOLF COURSE IN IRELAND
THE CURRAGH GOLF CLUB, KILDARE, IRELAND. 1856

The first golf course in Ireland was the Curragh. In 1852 the Earl of Eglinton, the Lord Lieutenant of Ireland and founder Captain of Prestwick Golf Club (1851) in Scotland, played golf on the Curragh with a Colonel Campbell of the Queens Bays. The previous year another native Scot (from Edinburgh) David Ritchie came to Ireland and claimed to have played golf 'with the late Mr Alexander Love on links he organized at Donnelly's Hollow at the Curragh, County Kildare in the early fifties'. When he died in 1910 Ritchie claimed to be the oldest golfer in Ireland.

However, despite claims in *The Guinness Book of Golf Facts and Feats*, the club is the second oldest in Ireland, but claims only to be the oldest golf course in Ireland dating back to an announcement in the *Irish Times* of 12 March 1883, 'Maj Gen Fraser V.C., C.B., Commanding the Curragh Brigade, has sanctioned the formation of a garrison golf club. The Rules of the Club will be the same as those of the Royal & Ancient Club of St Andrews, Scotland.' The present club has no records of either the course or the Club before 1887, a year when there were 11 holes. By 1889 there was a course that contained 18 holes. On 24 September 1910 it became the Royal Curragh. The Curragh Camp was evacuated by the British Army on 16 May 1922 and handed over to the Irish Defence Forces.

THE FIRST
GOLF CLUB ON
CONTINENTAL EUROPE

Pau Golf Club, Rue de Golf, 64140 Pau-Billere, Pau, France. 1856

The first golf club on continental Europe was the Pau Golf Club. It now stands on the delightfully named Rue de Golf. The second club, Biarritz Le Phare, was not founded until 1889. The first golfers at Pau were soldiers from the Duke of Wellington's regiment who were billeted there for the Battle of Orthez in February 1814. Two Scottish officers decided that the area in the shadow of the Pyrenees would make a terrific course and came to an agreement with local landowners to build a course. The club was all but abandoned during the First World War – most of its members were British – and all but collapsed during the Second World War. It was not until 1960 that the club once again thrived. It is known as 'the St Andrews of Europe' because of its lack of undulation.

THE FIRST
GOLFING MANUAL
SCOTLAND. 1857

H. B. Farnie's *The Golfer's Manual: Being an Historical and Descriptive Account of the National Game Of Scotland* was the first of its kind. It appeared under the pseudonym, "A Keen Hand". Henry Brougham Farnie (1836–1889) was a British librettist who also adapted French operettas for the London stage. For a time, Farnie's works competed in popularity with Gilbert and Sullivan, however, they have not stood the test of time. In 1914 *The Times* said that, 'The spoken dialogue was a kind of Sahara between the oases of song ... the attempts to fit English words to French music usually resulted in absolute nonsense.' Farnie was also the author of the *Handy Book of St Andrews*, which was a tome on the flora of the area.

THE FIRST
PLAYER TO BREAK 80 ON THE OLD COURSE AT ST ANDREWS
ALLAN ROBERTSON, OLD COURSE AT ST ANDREWS, SCOTLAND. WEDNESDAY 15 SEPTEMBER 1858

The game's first recognized professional (although that title did not exist at the time), Allan Robertson went round the Old Course at St Andrews in 79 strokes. Robertson, born 11 September 1815 at St Andrews, Fife, had the game in his blood. His father David was a weaver and golf-ball maker and, when his father died in 1836, Allan Robertson took over the family business that was run from the family home overlooking the links in Golf Place, St Andrews.

Robertson sold 1,021 featheries in 1840 and increased his output to 2,456 in 1844. His balls were always slightly cheaper than those sold by others. He was also a popular caddie, teacher and playing partner at St Andrews. The era of Allan Robertson was before the time of The Open but he was undefeated by many of his contemporaries and in June 1853 the *Fifeshire Journal* called him 'the real legitimate and indisputable King of Clubs'.

When the gutta-percha ball was invented, Robertson and his employee Tom Morris refused to use it fearing it would destroy the featherie business. The two men fell out and Morris started his own firm making gutta-percha balls only for Robertson to realize his error and follow suit. He played in various big money matches but only in foursomes and rarely singles. In 1853 he was elected captain of the St Andrews Golf Club.

There were some who believed that Tom Morris was a better player and they competed in two matches in September 1858, when each claimed a victory by one hole. It was during one of these matches that Robertson achieved the first ever score under 80 at St Andrews. Robertson died just under a year later on 1 September 1859 from jaundice at his home in Golf Place, St Andrews, Fife. Of him the Royal & Ancient Club said that he was 'a golfer who was never equalled in his life and has never been surpassed since his death'.

THE FIRST

AMATEUR GOLF CHAMPIONSHIP
St Andrews. 1859

George Condie of Perth won the first unofficial amateur championship. The third great tournament at St Andrews (1859) was won by George Condie, Perth, who defeated Sir Robert Hay.

THE FIRST

PROFESSIONAL GOLF TOURNAMENT
THE OPEN AT 2 LINKS ROAD, PRESTWICK, STRATHCLYDE, SCOTLAND. WEDNESDAY 17 OCTOBER 1860.

A year after the first amateur championship was held, the professionals took their turn with The Open at Prestwick. This course had opened in 1851 after a group of men met a local pub, the Red Lion, and decided to build a golf course. Eight Scottish golfers entered and Willie Park of Musselburgh won the title with a score of 174 over 36 holes, beating the favourite, Old Tom Morris, by two strokes.

The club members subscribed £25 to buy a red morocco belt with silver clasps to be presented to the winner. The first Open was played over three rounds of a 12-hole course in one day. A stone cairn to the west of the clubhouse marks the first tee. The first hole measured 578 yards (528 m) to what is now the 16th green. Seven of the original greens are still played on today.

Despite being called The Open, entry was limited to professionals and it was not until 1861 that it was indeed opened to all contestants, professional and amateur. That year it was won by Old Tom Morris (1821–1908). The following year, Old Tom Morris won by 13 strokes, which is still the largest winning margin. On 18 September 1863 prize money (a fund of £10) was introduced and two years later on 14 September 1865 official score cards made their first appearance.

On 23 September 1868 Young Tom Morris won, aged 17, and is still the youngest winner. In 1872 the competition became the responsibility of the Prestwick Club, Royal & Ancient Club of St Andrews and the Honourable Company of Edinburgh Golfers. The next year it was held at St Andrews, the first occasion away from Prestwick. In 1892 The Open was played over four rounds of 18 holes for the first time. In 1920 the Royal & Ancient Club of St Andrews took over sole responsibility.

THE FIRST
WOMEN'S GOLF CLUB

The Ladies' Golf Club at St Andrews, Fife, Scotland. 1867

The first golf club for women was formed at St Andrews. It was standard practice in those days for women to be allowed to play on the course only on days that men were not permitted.

THE FIRST
RECORDED HOLE-IN-ONE
Young Tom Morris at The Open, 2 Links Road, Prestwick, Strathclyde, Scotland. Monday 14 September–Thursday 17 September 1868.

During The Open held at Prestwick, Young Tom Morris (1851–1875) scored the first recorded hole-in-one on the 166-yard 8th hole. At 17 years and 249 days old, he became the youngest winner of the tournament. His father had been the oldest winner in 1867 at the age of 46 years and 99 days. Young Tom had shown great promise, winning £15 when he was just 13 in an exhibition match at Perth.

However, his was not to be a story with a happy ending. In the autumn of 1875, while playing an exhibition match in North Berwick with his father against Willie and Mungo Park, he received a telegram informing him that his wife of a year and newborn son had died on 4 September. He never got over their deaths and died on Christmas Day 1875, aged just 24. It was said that he passed away of a broken heart. The official cause of death was a pulmonary haemorrhage. A plaque inscribed in his memory at St Andrews Cathedral reads:

'Deeply regretted by numerous friends and all golfers, he thrice in succession won the championship belt and held it without rivalry and yet without envy, his many amiable qualities being no less acknowledged than his golfing achievements.'

THE ONLY
FATHER AND SON TO TAKE
THE TOP TWO PLACES IN A MAJOR COMPETITION
OLD TOM MORRIS AND YOUNG TOM MORRIS AT THE OPEN, 2 LINKS ROAD, PRESTWICK, STRATHCLYDE, SCOTLAND. THURSDAY 16 SEPTEMBER 1869

The year that Young Tom Morris won The Open for the first time, his father, Old Tom Morris (1821–1908), was the runner-up. Father and son each won The Open title four times. Old Tom Morris scored 157 and Young Tom went round in 154.

THE FIRST
GOLF CLUB IN AUSTRALIA
The Adelaide Golf Club, Adelaide, South Australia, Australia. June 1870

The first club 'down under' was The Adelaide Golf Club founded in the summer of 1870. However, it lasted only a few short years and is not related to the Royal Adelaide Golf Club, which was formed following a meeting held at the Largs Pier Hotel on 11 August 1892. Later that same year, on 8 October, its first competition was held on a course on the North Parklands. It became the Royal Adelaide Golf Club in 1923.

THE FIRST
AREAS FOR TEEING OFF
1870.

Prior to 1870 players would begin their assault on the next hole from the green of the hole that they had just completed. It is believed that separate areas for teeing off away from the green were introduced in 1870.

THE FIRST
PLAYER TO WIN
THE OPEN ON FRIDAY THE 13TH
YOUNG TOM MORRIS AT 2 LINKS ROAD, PRESTWICK, STRATHCLYDE, SCOTLAND. WEDNESDAY 23 SEPTEMBER 1868; THURSDAY 16 SEPTEMBER 1869; THURSDAY 15 SEPTEMBER 1870; FRIDAY 13 SEPTEMBER 1872

Young Tom Morris won The Open in 1868, 1869, 1870 and 1872; all four championships were played at Prestwick. There was no Open in 1871 because of an argument over a new trophy. In 1869 he scored 154, beating his father by three strokes. In 1870 he had a 12-stroke victory over Bob Kirk (in a 36-hole format), a stroke average that would not be equalled until the invention of the rubber-cored ball. In 1872 he hit 166, beating David Straith by three strokes. In that year Old Tom Morris came equal fourth with 179 strokes.

When Young Tom won the title in 1872 he was given the championship red morocco belt with silver clasps to keep. His belt is now in the keeping of the Royal & Ancient Golf Club of St Andrews. It was replaced by the current trophy, the Golf Champion Trophy, familiarly known as the Claret Jug. It was made by Mackay Cunningham & Company of Edinburgh and was hallmarked 1873.

YOUNG TOM MORRIS WAS ALSO: The FIRST name engraved on the Claret Jug, although the FIRST to be presented with the trophy was the 1873 winner Tom Kidd • The ONLY player to win four consecutive Opens

THE FIRST
OCCASION THE OPEN WAS HELD
ON OLD COURSE AT ST ANDREWS
THE OPEN AT OLD COURSE AT ST ANDREWS, FIFE, SCOTLAND.
SATURDAY 4 OCTOBER 1873

After a dozen Opens at Prestwick, the tournament was played for the first time on the Old Course at St Andrews. In the days leading up to The Open, St Andrews was hit by torrential rain, which left huge puddles on much of the course. If a player moved the ball from a puddle, he was subjected to a one-stroke penalty. Local caddie Tom Kidd won the 36-hole competition at his home course with a score of 179 (91 and 88), one fewer than Jamie Anderson, who also played at St Andrews. The penalties for the water traps meant that the winning score of 179 was the highest until the event was increased to 72 holes in 1892. Kidd won £11 for his Open triumph and died of heart disease in 1884.

THIS TOURNAMENT WAS ALSO NOTABLE FOR: Kidd being the FIRST golfer to use ribbed irons to impart backspin and beat a field of 26

THE FIRST
OCCASION THE OPEN
WAS HELD AT MUSSELBURGH

The Open at Musselburgh Links, the Old Golf Course, Balcarres Road, Musselburgh, East Lothian, Scotland. Friday 10 April 1874

After the success of the tournament away from Prestwick, The Open moved location again in 1874 – the 14th competition. The majority of the 32 players were locals but a good many arrived from St Andrews. The Open began at midday after it stopped raining although a strong wind blew throughout the four rounds of nine holes. Willie Park, the first Open champion in 1860, was paired with Young Tom Morris but neither was at his best and both players completed the first 18 holes in 83. Willie's younger brother, Mungo Park, won his first Open title with a score of 159 beating Young Tom by two strokes.

THE FIRST
OPEN WINNER BY DEFAULT

BOB MARTIN, THE OPEN AT OLD COURSE AT ST ANDREWS, FIFE, SCOTLAND. SATURDAY 30 SEPTEMBER 1876

A local golfer, Bob Martin, won the second Open Championship held at St Andrews by default when the joint leader Davie Strath refused to take part in a play-off. Martin went round in 86 and 90, which meant that Strath had to play the last two holes in 10 strokes to take The Open championship. His third shot on the 17th hit a player from a previous group rather than going past the green. However, on the 18th and last hole Strath took six shots to tie with Martin.

A complaint was made about Strath's behaviour on the 17th hole (hitting a fellow competitor) and the committee of the Royal & Ancient decided that no decision would be made until the two players had participated in a play-off. Understandably, Strath wanted a decision to be made before the play-off. When the committee refused to change their decision, Strath refused to take part, believing that it was possible he could win the play-off then be stripped of the title by the committee. Bob Martin walked The Old Course to become champion by default. Davie Strath died aged just 39 during a trip to Australia in 1879.

THE FIRST
OXBRIDGE VARSITY
GOLF MATCH
Wimbledon, London. 1878

The oldest club match in the world, between the two venerable universities Oxford and Cambridge, began with a victory for the dark blues of Oxford. The match was played on Wimbledon Common, courtesy of the London Scottish Golf club, by four singles over eighteen holes, using the holes up method of scoring.

THE FIRST
OPEN WINNER BY
PLAY-OFF
WILLIE FERNIE, THE OPEN AT MUSSELBURGH LINKS, THE OLD GOLF COURSE, BALCARRES ROAD, MUSSELBURGH, EAST LOTHIAN, SCOTLAND. SATURDAY 17 NOVEMBER 1883

The first play-off in The Open was scheduled for 1876 but one of the players, Davie Strath, refused to participate. The first play-off that actually took place was seven years later when Willie Fernie and Bob Ferguson tied on 159 (some sources list 158) strokes. Ferguson had won the previous three Opens and was looking for his fourth title. The greens were in good condition and, for once, in spite of the fact that it was winter in Scotland, the weather was warm and windless. On 16 November the competitors played four rounds of the nine-hole course. After two rounds, Fernie led Ferguson by 3 strokes and Willie Park Jr by 2. Fernie's luck ran out in the latter rounds and he and Ferguson finished level despite Ferguson playing nearly all of the last holes in partial darkness.

The next day, they met in a 36-hole play-off. Although Ferguson was the favourite to win, Fernie kept level with him. On the last hole, Ferguson was one stroke ahead but Fernie holed his ball in two. Needing to level, Ferguson missed his putt and Fernie won the play-off and The Open by one stroke.

THE FIRST

AMATEUR

CHAMPIONSHIP

THE AMATEUR CHAMPIONSHIP AT ROYAL LIVERPOOL GOLF CLUB, 30 MEOLS DRIVE, HOYLAKE, WIRRAL, ENGLAND. MONDAY 20-THURSDAY 23 APRIL 1885

The first championship teed off in the spring of 1885 but was not recognized as the start until much later. It was begun by the Royal Liverpool Golf Club as a 'tournament open to all amateur golfers'. An unusual aspect was the decision that halved matches would be replayed rather than decided on an extra hole. Forty-eight golfers entered and because there were no byes in the First Round, the first Amateur Championship had three players in the semi-final.

The first champion was Allen MacFie who had received a bye into the final and won by 7 and 6 over Horace Hutchinson. MacFie was lucky to get that far – he had halved two matches in the fourth round with Walter de Zoete and did not win until their third meeting, albeit on the last green. At the 13th he hit a hole-in-one, the first recorded in the competition. Horace Hutchinson had his revenge by winning in 1886 (the first officially recognized championship held at St Andrews, at which there were 44 entries but two were disqualified for being professionals), and 1887 (again at Hoylake; there were only 33 entries).

THE FIRST

GOLF CLUB IN AFRICA

THE ROYAL CAPE GOLF CLUB, WYNBERG, SOUTH AFRICA. 1885

The Royal Cape Golf Club, founded at a military base at Wynberg, South Africa, was the first club in Africa. It was given its Royal title in 1910 after a visit by the Duke of Connaught.

THE FIRST

GOLF COURSE IN THE USA

ST ANDREWS GOLF COURSE, YONKERS, NEW YORK, USA.
WEDNESDAY 14 NOVEMBER 1888

The first golf course in the USA was opened by John G. Reid in a field in Yonkers that had originally been home to cows. The club continues to thrive in Hastings-On-Hudson, just outside New York city.

THE FIRST

MIXED FOURSOME IN THE USA

Grey Oaks Course at St Andrews Golf Course, Yonkers, New York, USA.
Saturday 30 March 1889

John Reid and his wife played the first mixed foursome in the USA against John B. Upham and Carrie Low at the Grey Oaks Course, that had been opened by Reid four months earlier.

THE FIRST

'BRIBED' PLAYERS IN THE OPEN

ANDREW KIRKALDY, THE OPEN AT MUSSELBURGH LINKS, THE OLD GOLF COURSE, BALCARRES ROAD, MUSSELBURGH, EAST LOTHIAN, SCOTLAND.
MONDAY 11 NOVEMBER 1889

The last Open held at Musselburgh began at 10.30 am on a bright winter Friday morning. The organizing committee decided that in order to prevent large numbers of players finishing their rounds in the dark they would offer golfers lagging behind a five-shilling 'bribe' not to play in the fourth round. As it was, some players finished by the light of adjacent street lamps and cards were marked by candlelight. A large crowd turned out to watch the tournament.

Andrew Kirkaldy was on course to win The Open as he approached the 14th green with a simple tap-in from an inch away from the cup. He fluffed it and finished on 155, the same as Willie Park who performed exceptionally well on his final five holes. In the play-off Park won the Claret Jug by 158 to 163.

Park and Kirkaldy met for the 36-hole play-off on the Monday watched by around 1,000 people. Kirkaldy hit his ball into a bunker on the first hole and then his putt stopped on the edge of the cup for almost 30 seconds before it dropped in. The lead changed during the play-off, first Park went ahead and then Kirkaldy before Park played a terrific final round and finished ahead of Kirkaldy by 5 strokes.

THIS OPEN ALSO INCLUDED: The LAST Open held at Musselburgh • The ONLY player to lose The Open after missing a one-inch putt

THE FIRST
PLAYER TO WIN THE
OPEN AND THE AMATEUR
CHAMPIONSHIP

JOHN BALL, AMATEUR CHAMPIONSHIP AT 2 LINKS ROAD,
PRESTWICK, STRATHCLYDE, 1888; THE OPEN AT 2 LINKS ROAD,
PRESTWICK, STRATHCLYDE, SCOTLAND.
THURSDAY 11 SEPTEMBER 1890

English amateur golfer John Ball was born 24 December 1861 at Hoylake, Cheshire, where his father owned the Royal Hotel, which became the headquarters of the Liverpool Golf Club when the course was laid out in 1869. Ball began playing golf when he was 16 and in 1878 entered The Open finishing sixth.

He became the first non-Scotsman and first amateur to win The Open Championship when he triumphed at Prestwick in 1890. He went round in 164 (82–82) to win by three strokes on what Dr Laidlaw Purves called 'a great day for golf'. Oddly, it was the same course where two years earlier he'd won the British Amateur Championship for the first time beating J. E. Laidlay 5 and 4 in the final. As well as winning The Open in 1890, Ball also won the Amateur Championship again at Hoylake and again beating J. E. Laidlay in the final, this time 4 and 3.

It was the second of his record-breaking eight wins: 1888; 1890; 1892 (he was joint runner-up in The Open, won by another Hoylake amateur, Harold Hilton); 1894 (Hoylake, in which he played a shot over the cross bunkers to the Dun – then the seventeenth – hole and won by a hole); 1899 (Prestwick, winning at the 37th hole against his great Scottish rival F. G. Tait); 1907 (St Andrews); 1910 (Hoylake, beating Collinson Charleton Aylmer by 10 and 9); and 1912 (Westward Ho!, beating Abe Mitchell at the 38th hole).

Ball served in the Boer War with the Denbighshire Yeomanry. He won the Irish Amateur Championship three times (1893, 1894 and 1899). From 1888 until 1891 he won the St George's Cup at Sandwich, which was then considered the amateur stroke play championship, and from 1902 until 1911 he played for England against Scotland. In 1907 he won a bet by using a black ball. Playing at Hoylake, he claimed that he could go round the course in fewer than 90 strokes without losing the ball in the thick fog that covered the course. He managed it in 81 by using the black ball that stood out more in the mist.

Shy and retiring, Ball shunned publicity about his achivements; he left the Royal Hotel at Hoylake and moved to Lygan-y-wern near Holywell, Flintshire with his spinster sister Elizabeth and their housekeeper Nellie Williams, whom he married in July 1932. John Ball died at Lygan-y-wern on 2 December 1940.

HE WAS ALSO: The FIRST non-Scotsman to win The Open

THE FIRST
RECORDED
BOGEY SCORE
COVENTRY GOLF CLUB, COVENTRY, ENGLAND.
WEDNESDAY 13 MAY 1891

Coventry Golf Club instituted the first bogey score. The score was invented by the club secretary Hugh Rotherham as the score a golfer would get if he played a perfect round at each hole. Rotherham called it a 'Ground Score' but Dr Thomas Brown (Browne in some sources), honorary Secretary of the Great Yarmouth Club, called the perfect golfer a 'Bogey Man' after a popular music hall song of the day 'Here Comes the Bogey Man' and labelled the score a bogey.

Because golfers can reach the green in fewer strokes through various innovations, bogey is now one over the par score for the hole. Players claimed that they were playing against Mr Bogey but at the United Services Club at Gosport all the members had military ranks so they named their imaginary opponent Colonel Bogey. This later became the name of a popular march by Kenneth Alford.

THE LAST

OPEN PLAYED OVER
36 HOLES

The Open at Old Course at St Andrews, Fife, Scotland.
Tuesday 6 October 1891

The last Open played over 36 holes was the seventh held at St Andrews. The purse was £28.50; Hugh Kirkaldy was the victor with a score of 166 (83–83) and won the first prize of £10. There was also a record entry of 82 players.

THE FIRST

GOLF CLUB TO
ADMIT WOMEN

SHINNECOCK HILLS, 200 TUCKAHOE ROAD, SOUTHAMPTON, LONG ISLAND, NEW YORK, USA. 1891

The club was built on an 80-acre piece of land bought for $2,500 close to the Long Island Railroad, east of the Shinnecock Canal. There were originally 44 members, all of whom paid $100 each. The 12-hole course was designed by Willie Davis of the Royal Montreal Club and was built in collaboration with Shinnecock tribe of First Nations Americans. The clubhouse, said to be the oldest in America, was designed by Stanford White and opened in 1892.

The following year, a ladies-only nine-hole course was opened. Six more holes were added to the main course in 1894 and in 1895 Shinnecock was one of the five founding members of the United States Golf

Association. On 18 July 1896 James Foulis won the second US Open, the first held at Shinnecock. Five years later, the ladies' course was closed to allow the main course to be redesigned. It was further redesigned in 1937 by William Flynn.

THIS CLUB IS ALSO: The **ONLY** course to have played host to the US Open in three different centuries, as well as in **1986, 1995** and **2004** • The **ONLY** golf course built by **First Nations Americans**

MURDER, MAYHEM AND MADNESS

The designer of the Shinnecock Hills Golf Club clubhouse Stanford White was a notorious philanderer and was later murdered by the irate husband of one of his discarded mistresses. White also designed mansions, clubs and Madison Square Garden, where he kept an apartment in the top of the building. In this apartment White had installed a red velvet swing on which numerous young ladies were said to have swung. One night he invited beautiful Pennsylvania-born model Evelyn Nesbit to his apartment for dinner, and then drugged and raped her. White quickly lost interest in Nesbit and she resumed an affair with heir to a multi-million dollar mine and railroad fortune Harry Kendall Thaw, a ne'er do well with a reputed taste for sexual chastisement using dog leads. Evelyn Nesbit was initially reluctant to become involved with Thaw fearing what he would do if he learned that she was a 'fallen woman'. In the end that was the least of her worries. Thaw took her to a remote farmhouse where he, too, raped her and then beat her with a dog lead. Eventually, he made an honest woman of her. On 25 June 1906 Mr and Mrs Thaw attended a production of *Mam'zelle Champagne* in the rooftop theatre of Madison Square Garden in New York. Also in the audience was Stanford White and during the finale, 'I Could Love A Million Girls', Thaw shot him in the face three times. Thaw was charged and tried twice: the first trial ended in a hung jury and at the second he was found not guilty by reason of insanity. Thaw was sent to the Matteawan State Hospital for the Criminally Insane in Fishkill, New York. He was freed in 1913, but in 1917 he was accused of sexually assaulting a teenage boy, again adjudged insane and locked up. He was released in 1924. Thaw died of a heart attack in Miami, Florida on 22 February 1947. He left $10,000 in his will to Evelyn Nesbit.

THE FIRST
OPEN AT MUIRFIELD

Duncur Road, Muirfield, Gullane, East Lothian, Scotland.
Thursday 22–Friday 23 September 1892

The Open moved to Muirfield as the Honorary Company of Edinburgh Golfers replaced their headquarters at Musselbugh with Muirfield. To encourage more competitors, the prize money was raised from £28 10s to £110, with an entry fee of 10 shillings. The winner in the first Open played over 72 holes was Harold Horsfall Hilton, who became the second amateur to triumph. Oddly, he also won the Claret Jug the first time The Open was held at Hoylake (in 1897). From 1860 until 1891 The Open was played over 39 holes in one day. From 1892, players competed in four rounds over two days. Just 100 spectators turned up to watch Hilton's victory (see 1911, page 90)

ALSO AT THIS CLUB: The FIRST Open played over 72 holes

THE ONLY
GOLF COURSE HOLE NAMED FOR THE LAST WITCH EXECUTED IN BRITAIN

'THE WITCH', 17TH HOLE, ROYAL DORNOCH GOLF CLUB, GOLF ROAD, DORNOCH, SCOTLAND. 1892

In 1727 Janet Horne became the last person to be executed for sorcery in Britain. The local populace believed that she had been possessed by the Devil because her daughter was born with deformed hands and feet, similar to a horse's feet. Her accusers said that Horne had ridden her daughter to Hell where the Devil had shoed her. Horne and her daughter were arrested but the daughter managed to escape. Horne was not so

---

ROCK DORNOCH

On 21 December 2000 the pop star Madonna had her son Rocco christened in Dornoch Cathedral, the day before she married film director Guy Ritchie at nearby Skibo Castle.

---

fortunate – she was stripped, tarred and put into a barrel, whereupon she was rolled through the town before being burned alive at the stake near the site of the golf course.

The ninth hole at Dornoch is called 'The Witch' and has a water feature, supposedly the pond into which Horne was thrown to prove she was a witch. The theory was that if the witch floated she was guilty, if she drowned she was innocent. Janet Horne floated and was left to her horrible fate.

It is believed that golf was played at Dornoch as early as 1616 although the present course was not established until 5 November 1877. The first 18-hole course was opened in 1892. Other holes have been given names including: The Dyke, The Valley, Long Hole, The Bents, Foxy, The Flagstaff, Struy and The Nile. The course was altered from time to time but on 12 August 1948 a new layout added five new holes to replace the former 13th, 14th, 15th, 17th and 18th, consigning Janet Horne to history once more. The course achieved Royal status in 1906. In 2007 Dornoch was named the third-best course outside the United States by *Golf Digest*.

THE FIRST
GOLF MATCH AT WHICH
AN ENTRANCE FEE WAS CHARGED
CAMBRIDGE, ENGLAND. 1892

The first time spectators paid cash to watch a match occurred in the ancient university town of Cambridge. The competing players were Douglas Rollard and Jack White.

THE FIRST
GOLF CLUB IN ARGENTINA

Lomas Golf Club. 1892

The first recorded golf club in Argentina was the Lomas Club, which had been introduced by Britons who lived there. The locals described the British golfers as 'devoted to a strange sort of amusement'.

THE FIRST
WOMEN'S GOLF CHAMPIONSHIP

LYTHAM & ST ANNES GOLF CLUB, LINKS GATE, LYTHAM ST ANNES, LANCASHIRE, ENGLAND, TUESDAY 13 JUNE 1893

Lady Margaret Rachel Scott (1874–1938), the daughter of John Scott, 3rd Earl of Eldon and the fourth of seven children, won the first Ladies' British Open Amateur Golf Championship after the formation of the Ladies' Golf Union of Great Britain and Ireland. Oddly, there were no competitors from Scotland in the first championship and nor would there be any until 1897.

Lady Margaret retained her title in 1894 (at Littlestone) and 1895 (at Portrush). In 1893 and 1894 she beat Isette Pearson, the founder and first Secretary of the Ladies' Golf Union, by 7 and 5 and 3 and 2 respectively. Three of her brothers were also keen golfers: Osmund was the runner-up in the Amateur Championship at Prestwick in 1905; Denys won the second Italian Open Amateur Championship by 4 and 3 over Osmund in 1906; and Michael won the Amateur Championship at Hoylake in 1933, the oldest player to do so. Lady Margaret gave up the game when she married Frederick Gustavus Hamilton-Russell, the son of the 8th Viscount Boyne, on 27 April 1897.

THE FIRST
18-HOLE GOLF COURSE
IN THE USA

CHICAGO GOLF CLUB, BELMONT, ILLINOIS, USA.
TUESDAY 18 JULY 1893

A group of Scottish immigrants brought the game to the east coast of America in the 1880s. In 1892 Charles Blair Macdonald (whose father was of Scottish ancestry although born at Niagara Falls, Ontario), persuaded some fellow golfers to create the Chicago Golf Club. At first they played off nine holes about 23 miles (37 km) west of Chicago's Union Station on the first course west of the Allegheny Mountains. In 1893, a full 18-hole course – the first in America – designed and built by Macdonald opened for play. The following year, the members bought a parcel of land in Wheaton where the club still stands today.

THE FIRST
OPEN IN
ENGLAND

THE OPEN AT ST GEORGE'S GOLF CLUB,
SANDWICH, KENT, ENGLAND.
MONDAY 11–TUESDAY 12 JUNE 1894

The St George's Golf Club was formed in 1887 and just five years later it was selected to host the Amateur Championship. In 1894 the Royal & Ancient Club decided to move The Open out of Scotland for the first time. To ensure there were enough Scottish players participating, the club negotiated special rail fares for north-of-the-border golfers. Only 14 took advantage of the offer but there were 21 Scots working at English clubs who travelled to Kent to play, making the field 94, an increase of 12 on the previous record held by St Andrews.

THE FIRST

ENGLISH PROFESSIONAL
TO WIN THE
OPEN

THE OPEN AT ST GEORGE'S GOLF CLUB, SANDWICH, KENT, ENGLAND. MONDAY 11–TUESDAY 12 JUNE 1894

As well as the first time The Open was played in England, it was also the first time the Claret Jug was won by an English professional – John Henry Taylor of Northam, North Devon. From 1894 until 1914 there were just five years in which either he, James Braid or Harry Vardon did not win The Open. Taylor and Braid were triumphant five times each and Vardon six and at least one of them finished in the top three. Taylor's last victory came at Hoylake in 1913 when he won by eight strokes. He won The Open again in 1895 to become the first Englishman to win it twice. St George's was opened in 1887 and is a par 70 course. Edward VII bestowed Royal status on the club in May 1902.

THE FIRST

US GOLFING
MAGAZINE

GOLFING. NEW YORK, USA. 1894

Entitled *Golfing*, it was the first journal devoted entirely to the game. A weekly magazine, it was edited and published in New York by William L. Dudley and cost 10¢ or $4 for an annual subscription.

THE FIRST

PUBLIC GOLF COURSE IN THE USA

VAN CORTLANDT PARK GOLF COURSE, BRONX, NEW YORK, USA. SATURDAY 6 JULY 1895

The first public golf course in the USA opened on 6 July 1895 in the 1,146-acre park located in the Bronx in New York City. It is the fourth-largest park in New York City.

THE FIRST

US AMATEUR OPEN

NEWPORT COUNTRY CLUB, 280 HARRISON AVENUE, NEWPORT, RHODE ISLAND, USA. THURSDAY 3 OCTOBER 1895

In 1894 there were two competitions that billed themselves as the National Amateur Championship. One was played at Newport Country Club on 3–4 September and was won by William G. Lawrence who beat Chicago golfer Charles Blair Macdonald by 188 to 189; the other on 13 October saw Laurence B. Stottard victorious at St Andrews Golf Club in Yonkers, New York. Thirty-two contestants played over 18 holes and the runner-up was again, remarkably, Charles Blair Macdonald. This state of affairs could not be allowed to continue so Macdonald called for an organization to oversee amateur golf in America.

On 22 December 1894 the Amateur Golf Association of the United States (later the United States Golf Association) was founded – its charter members were Newport Golf Club, Shinnecock Hills Golf Club, the Country Club (Brookline, Massachusetts), St Andrew's Golf Club (Yonkers, New York.), and Chicago Golf Club – the first president was

Theodore A. Havemeyer of Newport Golf Club. It was the first national governing body for golf in the USA. In 1895 they arranged both the US Amateur Open and the US Open championships. The tournaments had been arranged originally for September but were delayed because of a clash with the-then more popular America's Cup yacht race. The first US Amateur champion turned out to be Charles Blair Macdonald, the man who had called for the organization in the first place. Macdonald beat Charles E. Sands by 12 and 11. In 1898 the US Amateur Championship was played on a different course and at a different time from the US Open for the first time.

THE FIRST

US OPEN

NEWPORT COUNTRY CLUB, 280 HARRISON AVENUE, NEWPORT, RHODE ISLAND, USA. FRIDAY 4 OCTOBER 1895

A year after an unofficial tournament at Yonkers, New York, which was won by American Willie Dunn, a 21-year-old Englishman Horace Rawlins (1874–1940), won the first official title by two shots over Willie Dunn. Ten professionals and one amateur entered the tournament. Rawlins, who scored 173 (91–82) with a gutta-percha ball, received $150 cash out of a total prize fund of $335, plus a $50 gold medal. Other monetary prizes were $100, $50 and $25. Rawlins's club was given The Open Championship Cup trophy, which was presented by the US Golf Association.

In 1898 the format of the US Open changed from two rounds (36 holes) to four (72 holes). By 1965 play was spread over four days. In 1912 more than a hundred players entered for the first time when the number reached 131. The number of entrants quickly increased after that with 265 in 1920, 696 in 1926, 1,064 just two years later in 1928, and it passed the 5,000 mark for the first time in 1982 when 5,255 competitors entered.

THE FIRST
WOMEN'S AMATEUR
GOLF CHAMPIONSHIP
IN THE USA

**MEADOW BROOK GOLF CLUB, WESTBURY, NEW YORK, USA.
SATURDAY 9 NOVEMBER 1895**

Almost 85 years after the first women's tournament was organized by the Musselburgh Golf Club in Scotland for the town's fishwives, the first competition for women was staged in Westbury, New York. The competition was unofficial and was won by Mrs Charles Stelle (Lucy Barnes) Brown who beat off 12 other players with a score of 132 (69–63) over 18 holes.

THE FIRST
BLACK GOLFER TO PLAY
IN THE US OPEN

John M. Shippen, Shinnecock Hills, 200 Tuckahoe Road, Southampton, Long Island, New York, USA. Saturday 18 July 1896

John Matthew Shippen Jr. was born in Washington DC in 1879, the son of a Presbyterian minister. When he was nine, his father Rev. John Shippen Sr. was sent to the Shinnecock First Nations Reservation (see 1891, page 53). The boy became a caddie on the course and when the location was chosen to host the second US Open, Shippen entered thanks to the generosity of the club members who paid his entrance fee and that of his friend Oscar Bunn, a Shinnecock First Nations American.

However, some of the white players threatened to boycott the tournament if Shippen and Bunn were allowed to compete. USGA president Theodore Havemeyer refused to be blackmailed and said that the competition would proceed even if Shippen and Bunn were the only contestants. The other players backed down. After a first round of 78 Shippen was tied for the lead but he blew his chance on the second round when he took 11 strokes to play the par-4 13th hole. He finished joint fifth with H. J. Whigham.

Shippen played five more times in the US Open and was the club professional at the Shady Rest Golf Course in New Jersey from 1924 to 1960. He also manufactured and sold his own clubs. He died in 1968 at Newark, New Jersey.

THE FIRST
WOMEN'S AMATEUR
MATCHPLAY GOLF CHAMPION
IN THE USA

**Beatrix Hoyt, Morris County Golf Club,
Morristown, New Jersey, USA. Friday
9 October 1896**

A year after the first woman's amateur championship, the competition format changed to matchplay and was won by Beatrix Hoyt who was just 16 at the time. The granddaughter of Chief Justice of the US Salmon P. Chase, she was a member of the Shinnecock Hills Golf Club in Southampton, New York. At Morris County Golf Club there were 29 entrants for eight places in the qualifying round. Hoyt returned the lowest score of 95. She won her Semi-Final by default over Anna Sands. In the Final she defeated Mrs Arthur Turnure 2–1. Beatrix Hoyt retained her title on 26 August 1897 and 16 October 1898 to become the first women's amateur matchplay golf champion for three consecutive years. She retired in 1900 at the age of 19. She died on 14 August 1963. Her achievement of three consecutive titles has been equalled but never bettered.

THE FIRST

COLLEGE GOLF ASSOCIATION IN THE USA

ARDSLEY CASINO GOLF CLUB, ARDSLEY-ON-HUDSON, NEW YORK, USA. JANUARY 1897

Students from Columbia, Harvard, Princeton and Yale formed the first intercollegiate golf association in America in 1897. On 13–14 May 1897 they held the first competition between the four colleges, and Yale triumphed in the team competition. Louis Pintard Bayard Jr. of Princeton won the individual title.

THE FIRST

AMATEUR TO WIN THE OPEN TWICE

Harold Hilton: The Open at Duncur Road, Muirfield, Gullane, East Lothian, Scotland. Thursday 22–Friday 23 September 1892; The Open at The Royal Liverpool Golf Club, 30 Meols Drive, Hoylake, Wirral, England. Wednesday 19–Thursday 20 May 1897

Harold Hilton, having triumphed at Muirfield in 1892 beating John Ball (the first amateur winner) by three strokes 305–308, became the first amateur to win The Open twice and did so on his home course of Hoylake. He beat James Braid by a single stroke 314–315. In third place was Freddie Tait, another amateur. Oddly, Hilton won The Open on the first occasion it was held at Muirfield and the first time it was held at Hoylake. Hilton would finish third in 1898, fourth in 1901, joint fifth in 1902 (also at Hoylake) but it would not be until 1926 that another amateur, Bobby Jones, would win The Open.

THE FIRST
PLAYER TO WIN
THE US AMATEUR
CHAMPIONSHIP TWICE

H. J. WHIGHAM, US AMATEUR CHAMPIONSHIP AT SHINNECOCK HILLS, 200 TUCKAHOE ROAD, SOUTHAMPTON, LONG ISLAND, NEW YORK, USA. 1896; US AMATEUR CHAMPIONSHIP AT CHICAGO GOLF CLUB, WHEATON, ILLINOIS, USA. 1897

A Renaissance man, Henry James Whigham (born at Tarbolton, Scotland on Christmas Eve 1869 and educated at Oxford), was invited by Charles Blair Macdonald to demonstrate golf at the 1893 Chicago World's Fair. In 1895 Whigham returned to Chicago where he taught English and economics at Lake Forest College. During his three-year tenure, he toured America taking part in several golf tournaments and winning the second and third US Amateur Championships. In 1896 he beat J. G. Thorp by 8 and 7 at Shinnecock Hills and the following year he beat W. R. Betts 8 and 6 at the Chicago Golf Club. In 1898 he left America to report on the Spanish-American War, to South Africa to cover the Boer War and then to China to write about the Boxer Rebellion. By 1907 he was back in America where he helped Macdonald design the National Golf Links of America. Whigham died at Southampton, New York on 17 March 1954.

THE FIRST
RULES OF GOLF
COMMITTEE
Royal & Ancient Club of St Andrews, Fife, Scotland. 1897

The game's first rules were drawn up on 7 March 1744. The committee was established in 1897 to oversee golf everywhere in the world apart from the USA and Mexico.

THE FIRST

GOLF COURSE TO USE
THE STABLEFORD
SCORING SYSTEM

GLAMORGANSHIRE GOLF CLUB, LAVERNOCK ROAD,
PENARTH, CARDIFF, WALES. 1898

In 1898, while a member of the Glamorganshire Golf Club, Dr Frank Barney Gordon Stableford created a scoring system to help golfers who were hindered by matters beyond their control. Born in 1870, he was a keen golfer with a handicap of one. He used the scores awarded by a normal bogey competition and used a points system to identify a winner but the experiment was not well-received so he abandoned it.

In 1907 he won the club championship at Royal Porthcawl. In 1914 he joined Wallasey Golf Club but soon left to answer his country's call during the First World War – he had previously served as a surgeon with the Royal Army Medical Corps in South Africa. When he returned to Wallasey at the cessation of hostilities his handicap had risen to eight. He became frustrated at the scoring system in place because the high winds at Wallasey made it almost impossible for a good golfer to go round in par or better.

To counter this, Stableford went back to the scoring system he had developed previously in Wales and modified it. As opposed to aiming for a low score, the winner under the Stableford method was the player with the highest score. It has some variations but the points awarded per hole as specified by the Royal & Ancient and the United States Golf Association are as follows: 2 or more over par – 0 points; 1 over par – 1 point; par – 2 points; 1 under – 3 points; 2 under – 4 points; etc. He said:

'I was practising on the second fairway at Wallasey Golf Club one day in the latter part of 1931 when the thought ran through my mind that many players in competitions got very little fun since they tore up their cards after playing only a few holes and I wondered if anything could be done about it.'

The first competition using the Stableford method took place at Wallasey on 16 May 1932. It proved instantly popular although very few professional tournaments adopted the method. One that did was the International although it was cancelled in February 2007 after 21 years. In 1969, ten years after his death, Wallasey donated The Frank Stableford Open Amateur Memorial Trophy. Henry Longhurst said of Stableford, 'I doubt whether any single man did more to increase the pleasure of the more humble club golfer.'

THE ONLY

WINNER OF THE US OPEN REQUIRED TO PAY A DEPOSIT FOR THE TROPHY

Fred Herd, US Open at Myopia Hunt Club, Off 435 Bay Road, South Hamilton, Massachusetts, USA. Friday 17–Saturday 18 June 1898

Like many golfers of his era, Fred Herd (1874–1954) liked a drink. He won the fourth US Open, which was held at the Myopia Hunt Club – the first US Open to be played over 72 holes. At the time Herd worked as a professional at the Washington Park course in Chicago. The Myopia Hunt Club course had only nine holes so players did the rounds eight times. He won the US Open by a clear seven strokes (328–335) over Alex Smith. However, such was Herd's reputation for enjoying a libation or three, that the organizing committee made him pay a deposit before they would allow him access to the trophy; they feared that he would pawn it to buy alcohol. His brother Sandy won The Open in 1902 at Hoylake.

THE FIRST
RUBBER-CORED
GOLF BALL

AKRON, OHIO, USA. TUESDAY 11 APRIL 1899

The first rubber-cored ball was designed and patented by Coburn Haskell of Cleveland, Ohio in 1899. Born in 1868, he moved to Cleveland from Boston, Massachusetts in 1892 and took a job with Marcus Hanna and the M. A. Hanna Company. Haskell's father was a close friend of Hanna and Coburn Haskell married Hanna's niece. Although an enthusiastic player of the game, Haskell did not set out to invent a new type of golf ball – his discovery was pure serendipity. Haskell had arranged a round with Bertram Work, then the superintendent of B. F. Goodrich at Akron, Ohio. Bertram had some work to do before the game so Haskell waited for him and picked up a piece of rubber and began playing with it. He wound it into a ball-shape and then tried to bounce it, only to find that it almost hit the ceiling. It was Work's idea when he saw what his friend had done to cover the ball. A year later, Haskell and Work took out a patent on their invention.

In 1901, Haskell retired from the M. A. Hanna Company and formed the Haskell Golf Ball Company to manufacture the new invention. That same year Walter Travis won his second US Amateur Championship becoming the first golfer to win a Major title with the Haskell ball. In 1902 Sandy Herd won the British Open and on 11 October of that year Laurie Auchterlonie triumphed in the US Open with the Haskell, causing virtually all players to switch.

Four years later, Goodrich introduced a rubber-cored ball but filled with compressed air and called the 'Pneu-matic' – the only problem was that in warm weather the ball had a tendency to explode, often while stored in a golfer's pocket. The Haskell ball continued its dominance when the Pneu-matic was taken off the market. In 1917 Haskell sold his company and patent. He died on 14 December 1922. In 2001, the B. F. Goodrich Company changed its name to the Goodrich Corporation.

THE FIRST
AMERICAN TO WIN
THE US AMATEUR
CHAMPIONSHIP

Herbert M. Harriman, Onwentsia Club, 300 North Green Bay Road,
Lake Forest, Illinois USA. Saturday 8 July 1899

Having seen a Canadian and two Scotsmen win the first four US Amateur
Championships, New York-born Herbert Harriman was determined to
break the foreign monopoly on the tournament. At the fifth championship
he beat Scotsman and reigning champion Findlay Douglas in the Final
by 3-2.

THE FIRST
GOLF TEE

BOSTON, MASSACHUSETTS, USA. TUESDAY 12 DECEMBER 1899.

American dentist George F. Grant patented the golf tee at the end of 1899.
Before Grant's innovation, golfers used a mix of water and sand or dirt to
build a small mound from which to tee off.

THE FIRST
USE OF THE TERM
'BIRDIE'

ATLANTIC COUNTRY CLUB, 1 LEO FRASER DRIVE, NORTHFIELD,
NEW JERSEY, USA. 1899

The term 'birdie' – meaning one under par for the hole – was first coined
at Atlantic Country Club. Abe (in some records Ab) Smith, his brother

William and George Crump were playing the second hole, which was a par four about 350 yards (320 metres) long. Abe Smith takes up the story:

'My drive of 185 yards [170 metres] was to the left giving me the diagonal of the green to play for. The green was guarded by a ditch and a cup bunker. I banged away with my second shot, and my ball, one of the new Haskells, came to rest within 6 inches [15 cm] of the cup. I said to Crump, "That was a bird of a shot and here I only get a paltry sum from each of you. Hereafter, I suggest that when one of us plays a hole in one under par that he receives double compensation, and this goes for everyone in the match including partners. The other two agreed and we began right away, just as soon as the next one came, to call it a birdie.'

THE ONLY
BRITISH AMATEUR CHAMPION
KILLED IN THE
BOER WAR

Freddie Tait at Koodoosberg, South Africa, Wednesday 7 February 1900

Frederick Guthrie Tait was born in Edinburgh on 11 January 1870, the third son of Peter Guthrie Tait (1831–1901), a professor of natural philosophy at Edinburgh University. In 1887 his eldest brother, John Guthrie Tait (1861–1945), was a beaten semi-finalist in the Amateur Championship. Three years later, at the Royal & Ancient Golf Club of St Andrews, Freddie Tait set an amateur record by going round in 77 and bested that in 1894 with a round of 72. It should be remembered that he was using a gutta-percha ball and course maintenance had yet to reach the standards that players expect today.

On 11 January 1893 at St Andrews playing against Guy Grindlay, Tait hit the ball 250 yards (228 metres) ; the ball then rolled on the icy ground and finished 341 yards (311 metres) from the tee. Tait won the British Amateur Champion in 1896 (beating Johnny Laidlay, John Ball, Horace Hutchinson and, in the final, Harold Hilton by 8–7 at Sandwich in the first 36-hole final) and again in 1898 at Hoylake when he won by 7–5 against Samuel Mure-Ferguson. Tait finished runner-up in 1899. In The

Open he was the highest finishing amateur in 1894, 1896 and 1899 and finished third in 1896 and 1897. He was also a keen cricketer and rugby player (he played for Edinburgh Wanderers).

After Royal Military Academy, Sandhurst (he is often credited with introducing golf to Sandhurst), he was gazetted to the 2nd Battalion, the Leinster Regiment (109th Foot). In June 1894 he was swapped with an officer and joined the 2nd Battalion, the Black Watch. It was as a member of the Black Watch Golf Club that he played in tournaments.

Tait was posted to South Africa with his regiment to join the Highland Brigade at the start of the Boer War. On 11 December 1899 he was wounded in the left thigh at Magersfontein. Having recovered, he was killed leading a charge of the Black Watch. He was just over a month past his 30th birthday. He was buried the next day on the bank of the Riet River near Koodoosberg. The Freddie Tait Cup is awarded annually to the leading amateur in the South African Open Championship.

THE FIRST

PLAYER TO WIN THE OPEN AND US OPEN

Harry Vardon, The Open at Duncur Road, Muirfield, Gullane, East Lothian, Scotland. Thursday 11 June 1896; the US Open at Chicago Golf Club, Wheaton, Illinois, USA. Friday 5 October 1900

Harry Vardon won the Claret Jug for the first time in 1896 beating J. H. Taylor in a play-off after both had scored 316. Four years later, he won the US Open and, remarkably, his vanquished opponent was again J. H. Taylor, although this time the winning margin was a more comfortable two strokes at 313–315.

THE FIRST

GOLF COURSE BUILT WITH GRASS GROWN FROM SEED

SUNNINGDALE, RIDGEMOUNT ROAD, ASCOT, BERKSHIRE, ENGLAND. 1901

Sunningdale was built on forested land in 1901 and its grass was grown entirely from seed. Previous courses had been built in and around meadows, which caused drainage problems because meadows were usually on top of clay soil. Two years earlier, brothers T. A. and G. A. Roberts built a house in Sunningdale called Ridgemount. Towards the end of that year, they decided to build a golf course and on 4 December 1899 the cost was agreed at £3,000. In February 1900 the club's first committee was formed and it was decided to make it a members-only club. The first Annual General Meeting of Sunningdale Golf Club was held at the Café Monico in London on 29 March 1900.

THE FIRST

US OPEN WINNER NOT TO DEFEND HIS TITLE

Harry Vardon, Myopia Hunt Club, Off 435 Bay Road, South Hamilton, Massachusetts, USA. Monday 15–Tuesday 16 July 1901

Born on the Channel island of Jersey on 9 May 1870 and one of eight children, Henry William 'Harry' Vardon began playing at his local course, the Royal Jersey Golf Club. Vardon was the first professional golfer to wear plus fours.

In 1890 he landed a job as pro at a new course at Studley Royal near Ripon in North Yorkshire. It was not long before he moved to Bury in Lancashire, where he was the professional until 1896 (three years after he first entered The Open), when he moved again to Ganton. In 1894 he finished sixth in The Open. Two years later in 1896 he won the Claret Jug for the first time beating J. H. Taylor in a play-off at Muirfield. Vardon won The Open five more times (at Prestwick in 1898, 1903 – when he suffered from tuberculosis and spent a long time recuperating at Mundesley Sanatorium in Norfolk – and 1914, and at Sandwich in 1899 and 1911); he was runner-up on four other occasions.

In 1900, a golfing superstar, he toured America and in October of that year won the US Open at the Chicago Golf Club, Illinois with a score of 313 (79–78–76–80). Such was the difficulty of travelling in those far-off days that Vardon did not play in the US Open again until September 1913, when he was second to 20-year-old amateur Francis Ouimet in a play-off. Vardon's last appearance in the US Open came in August 1920 when he tied for second place behind fellow Englishman Ted Ray.

Vardon was nicknamed the 'Napoleon of Golf' and the 'Greyhound'. He developed the overlapping grip named after him and a more upright swing as well as designing 14 courses and writing *The Complete Golfer*, which went through 13 editions from 1905 until a revised edition was published in 1914. On 15 November 1891 he married the pregnant Jessie Bryant who gave birth to his son Clarence Henry in June 1892. The boy died on 5 August and in 1896 Jessie suffered a miscarriage. Mrs Vardon took little interest in her husband or his career and he found solace in the arms of Tilly Howell, a dancer 22 years his junior, who bore him a son on 23 January 1926.

The most recent winner not to defend his title was Payne Stewart, tragically killed in an aeroplane crash four months after his win in June 1999.

THE FIRST

PLAY-OFF IN
THE US OPEN
MYOPIA HUNT CLUB, OFF 435 BAY ROAD, SOUTH HAMILTON, MASSACHUSETTS, USA. TUESDAY 16 JULY 1901

Having been expanded to 72 holes in 1898, the seventh US Open was the first to require a play-off to decide the champion. After four rounds Willie Anderson and Alex Smith were both tied on 331 strokes. Anderson had gone round in 84–83–83–81 while Smith had 82–82–87–80. The play-off was equally tight with Anderson winning by just one stroke – 85–86. In 1902 Anderson finished a poor sixth but his best was yet to come (see 1905, page 82).

THE FIRST
GOLF COURSE IN JAPAN

MOUNT ROKKO, NEAR KOBE, JAPAN. 1901

The first course in Japan consisted of nine holes on the slopes of Mount Rokko. The game was introduced by a group of Englishmen, led by merchant Arthur Hesketh Groom, who found judo too violent for their tastes. Although the first recorded native winner was Inoe Shin in 1918, the Japanese did not really take to the game until the 1920s and 1930s, but the Second World War intervened and it was 1952 before requisitioned golf courses were returned to their rightful owners.

THE FIRST
OPEN WIN WITH THE HASKELL BALL

The Open at The Royal Liverpool Golf Club, 30 Meols Drive, Hoylake, Wirral, England. Thursday 5 June 1902

In 1902 Sandy Herd won The Open by one shot with a score of 307 (77–76–73–81) using the new Haskell ball. Herd was also the first recorded golfer to waggle his club as he addressed the ball. He first entered The Open in 1885 and his last appearance was in 1939 when he was 71.

THE FIRST
PLAYER TO SHOOT FEWER THAN 80 IN ALL FOUR ROUNDS OF THE US OPEN

LAURIE AUCHTERLONIE, US OPEN AT GARDEN CITY GOLF CLUB, 206 STEWART AVENUE, GARDEN CITY, NEW YORK, USA. SATURDAY 11 OCTOBER 1902

Helped by the Haskell rubber-cored ball, Laurie Auchterlonie won the US Open by becoming the first player to score fewer than 80 in all four rounds. He scored a total of 307 made up of 78–78–74–77.

THE FIRST
STEEL-SHAFTED GOLF CLUB

SCHENECTADY, NEW YORK, USA. TUESDAY 24 MARCH 1903

General Electric engineer Arthur F. Knight patented the first steel-shafted club (with an aluminium putter) after finding the current clubs did not meet his needs. He played at the Mohawk Golf Club at Schenectady, New York and soon received an order for the new-fangled device from Walter J. Travis, a leading amateur golfer. Travis used the club (and was quoted as saying it was 'the best putter I have ever used') when he came third in the US Open held at Garden City Golf Club at New York on 10–11 October 1902. Travis used the putter to win the 1903 US Amateur and then the 1904 Amateur championships. These clubs were banned by the committee of the Royal & Ancient Club of St Andrews in 1910 but were permissible in America. The clubs were not manufactured in Britain until 1929 when Spaldings of Putney, London began making them after they were used by the then Prince of Wales.

THE FIRST

FATHER AND SON(S) TO PLAY IN THE US OPEN

Tom Anderson Sr. and Tom Anderson Jr. and Willie Anderson at Baltusrol Golf Club, 201 Shunpike Road, Springfield Township, Union County, New Jersey, USA. Saturday 27 June 1903

Rather than just a father and son combination playing in the US Open, 1903 saw the first and, to date, only father and sons competing. It would be 44 years before another father and son played in the same US Open – Willie and Mac Hunter competed in 1947 at the St Louis Country Club in Missouri.

The Andersons were a family of golfers – father Tom was green keeper on the North Berwick West Links but by the beginning of the 20th century Tom and his two sons were all living in America.

In 1903 all three entered the US Open at Baltusrol, the competition that son Willie had won in 1901. In 1903 he won it again beating David 'Deacon' Brown in a play-off. During the play-off Willie Anderson said barely a word to Brown all day. He beat him by two shots. A fellow competitor Fred McLeod recalled, 'When you played golf with him, you played golf. He would even tell you on the first tee, "We're the best of friends, but friendship ceases right here." When you played him if he was 1 up he wanted to be 2 up and if he was 2 up he wanted 3. If he beat you he was the nicest fellow in the world.'

All three family members would be dead within 13 years of their achievement. Willie Anderson died, aged just 31, in 1910. His father died three years later and in 1915 the younger Tom Anderson was killed in a car crash. They are buried together in Chestnut Hill Cemetery, Philadelphia.

THE FIRST

PLAYER TO BREAK 70
AT THE OPEN

**JAMES BRAID, THE OPEN AT THE ROYAL ST GEORGE'S GOLF CLUB,
SANDWICH, KENT, ENGLAND. WEDNESDAY 8–FRIDAY 10 JUNE 1904**

Born at Liberty Place, Elie, Fife on 6 February 1870, James Braid was the son of a ploughman who became a forester. Braid took to golf early as a caddie and then as a player, winning boys' competitions. He left school at 13, keen to become a golfer, an ambition not shared by his parents who apprenticed him to a joiner in a neighbouring village. Braid played golf on summer evenings and Saturday afternoons but that was enough to win him the scratch medal of the Earlsferry Thistle Golf Club with a record score when he was 16.

Three years later, he found a job as a joiner at St Andrews, which gave him more time to practise his golf. At 21, Braid relocated to Edinburgh and joined the Edinburgh Thistle Club, where he won the amateur competition open to all Edinburgh golfers.

In the autumn of 1893 Braid moved to London, where he took a job as a club maker at the Army and Navy Stores in London at the suggestion of his boyhood friend Charles Ralph Smith, who was then the senior club maker. Braid worked for the Army and Navy for almost three years and spent his weekends on golf courses.

In 1894 he played in his first open professional competition at Stanmore and finished fifth. Later that summer, he played in The Open for the first time. He finished a respectable tenth. From 1896 until 1904 Braid was professional at Romford in Essex. After eight years, he was appointed the first professional at Walton Heath, where he stayed for the rest of his life. In 1897 at Hoylake, he finished second in The Open to Harold Hilton, beaten by one stroke. Four years later, he won the Claret Jug for the first time with a score of 309 at Muirfield.

It was around this time that Braid's name became forever linked with those of Harry Vardon and J. H. Taylor as the Triumvirate of British golfers who would dominate the game. In the third round of The Open in 1904 Braid went round in 69, becoming the first player to break 70 in the competition. In the fourth round, J. H. Taylor went one better, and in the same round the eventual winner Jack White equalled Braid's score.

In 1905 and 1906 Braid won The Open although the nearest he came to breaking 70 was in the fourth round in 1906 when he scored 73. He won the Claret Jug again in 1910 and in the second round again scored 73. He was thus Open champion four times in six years. Braid also won the *News of the World* tournament in 1903, 1905, 1907 and 1911, and the French championship in 1910. His eyesight, never good after lime was thrown accidentally into his eyes when he was a boy, deteriorated and he began working as a golf-course architect.

James Braid died in a nursing home at 31 Queen's Gate, London on 27 November 1950, after an operation.

THE LAST
APPEARANCE OF GOLF AT THE OLYMPICS

ST LOUIS, MISSOURI, USA. SATURDAY 24 SEPTEMBER 1904

Women's golf only appeared in the Olympics once, at Paris-Compiegne, France in 1900. The Gold Medal was won by Margaret Abbott who amazingly did not even realize that she was participating in the Olympics, so poor were the organizational skills of the French. Abbott, a 22-year-old art student from Chicago, Illinois, was under the impression that she was playing in the French Women's Amateur Championship. Abbott went round the nine-hole course in 47 strokes. Her mother was also competing and finished joint seventh with a score of 63. Margaret Abbott was the first American woman to win an Olympic Gold (on 3 October 1900) and she said that she had won 'because all the French girls apparently misunderstood the nature of the game and turned up to play in tight skirts and high heels'.

Americans took the top three places and were also placed fifth and seventh. On 10 December 1902, Abbott married political satirist Finley Peter Dunne; she died on 10 June 1955, still unaware that she had competed in the Olympics. The day before her victory, Charles Sands of the USA had won the men's Gold Medal – he also took part in the tennis competition that year but was not placed.

On 17 September 1904, the Americans took the Gold, Silver and Bronze medals in the St Louis games. A week later, George Lyon won the last golfing Olympic Gold. Born at Richmond, Ontario, Canada on 27 July 1858 George Seymour Lyon was a keen sportsman who played baseball, cricket and tennis. In 1876, he set a Canadian pole vault record and he captained Canada at international cricket. His highest score was reported to be an undefeated 234 (some sources say 238).

At the age of 38, Lyon picked up his first golf club. Between 1898 and 1914, he won the Canadian Amateur title eight times – 1898, 1900, 1903, 1905, 1906, 1907, 1912 and 1914. At the age of 46, he travelled from Toronto to St Louis to play in the Olympics. He caused amusement and bewilderment in equal measure during the competition. He sang, told jokes and even did handstands on the course but also shocked some purists with his grip, which was more like that used on a cricket bat or, according to a New York columnist like 'using a scythe to cut wheat'. A 75-player field was whittled down to 32 and the survivors contested a matchplay competition. In the Semi-Final, Lyon defeated Francis Newton and in the Final he beat H. Chandler Egan by 3 and 2. Lyon was presented with a $1,500 sterling silver trophy, which he collected by walking to the podium on his hands.

In 1906 Lyon was runner-up to Eben Byers in the US Amateur Championship by 2-up. Two years later, Lyon travelled to London to defend his title but British golfers argued among themselves and decided to boycott the Games, which mean that Lyon was the sole entrant. The Olympic organizing committee offered Lyon the Gold Medal by default but he refused to accept it. Lyon died at Toronto, Ontario on 11 May 1938. He was inducted into Canada's Sports Hall of Fame in 1955 and 16 years later into the Canadian Golf Hall of Fame.

Golf is making a comeback at the Olympics and golfers from many countries will compete in the 2016 Olympics at Rio de Janeiro, Brazil.

THE FIRST

NON-BRITON
TO WIN THE
AMATEUR CHAMPIONSHIP

WALTER TRAVIS AT THE ROYAL ST GEORGE'S GOLF CLUB, SANDWICH, KENT, ENGLAND. 1904

Walter J. Travis, born in Australia but living in America, became the first non-British player to win the Amateur Championship, triumphing at Royal St George's beating Ted Blackwell 4–3 in the final. It was the only time that he competed in the tournament. He did not make the cut at The Open that year, again his only attempt at the competition. He would be the only American to win until 1926 when Jess Sweetser won at Muirfield.

Travis became an American citizen in 1890 but did not begin playing golf until he was almost 35 and consequently was nicknamed 'the Old Man'. It was a visit to England that inspired his interest in golf. He had played cricket and tennis as a young man without any success. He won his first tournament, the Oakland Golf Club handicap at Bayside, Long Island, a month later, acquiring a much-cherished pewter tankard. In 1898 Travis participated in the US Amateur Championship for the first time and lost to Findlay S. Douglas in the Semi-Final. He competed in 17 consecutive US Amateur Championships winning in 1900 (at the Garden City Golf Club, Long Island beating Findlay S. Douglas 2 up), 1901 (at Atlantic City, New Jersey beating W. E. Egan by 5–4) and 1903 (at Nassau New York defeating E. M. Byers by 5–4). Travis retired in 1916 as his heath began to fail.

As well as being a golfer, Travis was also a journalist, an author (he wrote *Practical Golf* in 1901 and *The Art of Putting* in 1904), a golf-course designer and mentor to many young players including Bobby Jones. In 1908, Travis founded and published the magazine *The American Golfer*. He died on 31 July 1927 at Denver, Colorado, where he had moved in the hope it would help his bronchial illness. In 1979 he was inducted into the World Golf Hall of Fame. Of his enthusiasm for the game, Travis wrote:

'Always be on the aggressive. Act as if you are quite sure of yourself and never give an opponent the psychological advantage of imagining you are the least afraid of him. Many a man is beaten before he starts by admitting to himself the other's fancied superiority and unconsciously conveying it in his general bearing. It only gives the opponent that slight encouragement which enables him to pull out a winner in a tight match. I am not aware of ever having possessed any physical advantages that enabled me to climb the ladder as I did in such a comparatively short space of time. What success I managed to achieve was primarily due to an intense love of the game, a devotion, which made practice not a drudgery but a pleasure. "Genius," I think it was Carlyle, who said, "is the capacity of taking infinite pains." I practised at every opportunity. Full as my cup has been, I shall never cease to regret the many prior years which were wasted.'

THE ONLY
PLAYER TO WIN
THE LADIES BRITISH OPEN
CHAMPIONSHIP
AND WIMBLEDON LADIES'
SINGLES TITLE

LOTTIE DOD, LADIES' SINGLES TITLE AT WIMBLEDON, LONDON, ENGLAND. JULY 1887. LADIES BRITISH OPEN CHAMPIONSHIP AT TROON, CRAIGEND ROAD, AYR, SOUTH AYRSHIRE, SCOTLAND. 1904

An all-round sportswoman, Charlotte 'Lottie' Dod won the Ladies British Open Championship at Troon by one hole over May Hezlet in 1904 before a crowd of around 5,000. Born at Lower Bebington, Cheshire on 24 September 1871, Dod was 15 when she won the Ladies' Singles title at Wimbledon for the first time – still the youngest ever winner. She beat Blanche Bingley 6–2, 6–0, winning the second set in just 10 minutes. She went on to win the competition five times (1888, beating Bingley again, this time 6–3, 6–3; 1891, beating Bingley 6–2, 6–1; 1892, beating, who else?, Bingley 6–1, 6–1; and 1893 again against Bingley 6–8, 6–1, 6–4).

Dod retired from competitive tennis after her last Wimbledon win, bored by the sport and keen to participate in other activities. She began playing golf and entered the 1894 Ladies' British Open Amateur Championship but was knocked out early. In February 1896, she climbed the 13,130 ft (4,000 metre) Piz Zupo and that winter also went down the Cresta Run. In 1898, she made it to the Semi-Finals of the Ladies' British Open Amateur Championship. In March 1899, she played hockey at inside right for England against Ireland at Richmond, where her skilful dribbling led to a 3–1 victory for England. In 1904, after winning the Ladies' British Open Amateur Championship she participated in the US Ladies' Championship but was defeated in the first round. In 1906, she turned her arm to archery and on 20 July 1908 she won Silver Medal in National Round archery at the Olympics (eldest brother William won gold in York Round archery at the same Games on 18 July). Oddly, he lived to be 87 but never went to school, never worked and never married. He was 39 before he took up archery and won the Gold Medal on his 41st birthday. He and Lottie were the first brother and sister to win Olympic medals. Both the contests in which they won medals have been discontinued.

She became president of the Royal North Devon Golf Club in 1949. She never married and died following a fall, at Birch Hill Nursing Home, Sway, Hampshire, on 27 June 1960, while listening to Wimbledon on the wireless.

THE ONLY
PLAYER TO WIN
THREE CONSECUTIVE
US OPEN TITLES

WILLIE ANDERSON, US OPEN AT BALTUSROL GOLF CLUB, 201 SHUNPIKE ROAD, SPRINGFIELD TOWNSHIP, UNION COUNTY, NEW JERSEY USA. SATURDAY 27 JUNE 1903; AT GLEN VIEW CLUB, 100 GOLF ROAD, GOLF, ILLINOIS, USA. SATURDAY 9 JULY 1904; AT MYOPIA HUNT CLUB, OFF 435 BAY ROAD, SOUTH HAMILTON, MASSACHUSETTS USA. FRIDAY 22 SEPTEMBER 1905

Born on 21 October 1879 at North Berwick, East Lothian, Scotland, Willie Anderson emigrated to the USA with his 23-year-old friend

FOUR TIMES A WINNER

Willie Anderson won his fourth and final US Open title in 1905 with a score of 81–80–76–77 for a total of 314. The runner-up was his fellow Scot Alex Smith who was also second when Anderson won his first US Open in 1901. Smith won his first title in 1906 (see page 84) when the runner-up was his brother Willie. Alex Smith won the title again in 1910 when one of the runners-up was his other brother Macdonald.

Thomas Warrender in March 1897 aboard the SS Pomeranian (27 of the 97 passengers did not survive the voyage, dying of 'ship fever'). He played in the US Open for the first time in September of that year at the Chicago Golf Club in Illinois, finishing second by one stroke after Joe Lloyd from Essex eagled the final hole.

In 1899 Anderson won the Southern California Open. Two years later, he won the US Open for the first time. Anderson is still the only man to have won three consecutive titles; only Bobby Jones (1923, 1926, 1929 and 1930; Ben Hogan (1948, 1950, 1951 and 1953) and Jack Nicklaus (1962, 1967, 1972 and 1980) have equalled his total of four championships. Anderson is the only player to win Opens with both the guttie and the rubber-cored ball.

On 17 September 1902, Anderson won his first Western Open at the Euclid Club in Cleveland, Ohio with an historic 299. No golfer had previously broken 300 for 72 holes in America. He won the 1903 title at Baltusrol Golf Club in New Jersey on a play-off 82–84 having scored 307 (149–79–82), the 1904 at Glen View Club, Illinois by five strokes, scoring 303 (75–78–78–72) and the 1905 at the Myopia Hunt Club in Massachusetts by two strokes, having scored 314 (81–80–76–77). In 1906 he ranked a disappointing fifth.

He died at Chestnut Hill, Philadelphia, Pennsylvania on 25 October 1910 aged just 31, officially from 'arteriosclerosis' or a heart attack, although some have posited that his death was due to alcoholism.

Anderson was an original member of the PGA Hall of Fame and was inducted into the World Golf Hall of Fame in 1975. He left a widow and baby but no trace of them was found and Gene Sarazen accepted the award on Anderson's behalf. Anderson's opponent Alex Smith said of him, 'Most likely, had he lived longer, Willie would have set a record for Open Championships that would never be beaten' (see 1901, page 73).

THE FIRST
PLAYER TO WIN
THE US OPEN IN
FEWER THAN 300 SHOTS
OVER 72 HOLES

Alex Smith, US Open at Onwentsia Club, 300 North Green Bay Road, Lake Forest, Illinois, USA. Friday 29 June 1906

Alex Smith recorded 295 (73–74–73–75) at the Onwentsia Club to win the US Open and take home $300 in prize money. He won by seven strokes, the biggest margin since 1899.

THE FIRST
HOLE-IN-ONE
AT THE US OPEN

JACK HOBENS AT PHILADELPHIA CRICKET CLUB, 415 WEST WILLOW GROVE AVENUE, PENNSYLVANIA, PHILADELPHIA, USA. FRIDAY 21 JUNE 1907

Jack Hobens scored the first hole-in-one during the US Open in 1907. He holed the 147 yard (134 metre) 10th hole in the second round. He finished the tournament in fourth place scoring 309 (76–75–73–85).

THE FIRST

CONTINENTAL EUROPEAN TO WIN THE OPEN

Arnaud Massey at The Royal Liverpool Golf Club, 30 Meols Drive, Hoylake, Wirral, England. Friday 21 June 1907

A man of many firsts, Frenchman Arnaud Massey won the first Open in his own country in 1906 (and retained it the following year); in 1910 he won the first Belgian Open and in 1912 he won the first Spanish Open. In 1907 at Hoylake, he became the first golfer from continental Europe to win the Claret Jug with a score of 312 (76–81–78–77).

THIS TOURNAMENT ALSO SAW: Massey become the ONLY Frenchman to win The Open • The FIRST time qualifying rounds were introduced at The Open

THE FIRST

LADY GOLF PROFESSIONAL

MRS GORDON ROBERTSON, PRINCES LADIES GOLF CLUB, MITCHAM COMMON, SURREY, ENGLAND. 1908

Very little is known about Mrs Gordon Robertson (not even her Christian name) but we know that she was the first lady professional, followed in 1911 by Lily Freemantle who was appointed professional to the Sunningdale Ladies' Club. It was not long afterwards that Mrs D. M. Smyth became the professional at Le Touquet Ladies' club.

THE FIRST

PLAYER TO BREAK 70 AT THE US OPEN

DAVID HUNTER, THE US OPEN AT ENGLEWOOD GOLF CLUB, ENGLEWOOD, BERGEN COUNTY, NEW JERSEY, USA. FRIDAY 25 JUNE 1909

David Hunter became the first player to score fewer than 70 in the US Open when he carded 68 on the morning of the 15th running of the tournament. Hunter peaked too soon and in the afternoon he scored 84 to finish 23 shots behind the winner George Sargent who set a record for tournament scoring with a 290 (75–72–72–71) – five shots better than any 72-hole US Open score before it. Only 84 players entered the tournament.

Almost as soon as the US Open left Englewood, the course began its slow decline. Considered one of the finest of its day, Englewood Golf Club had played host to the then more prestigious US Amateur Championship in 1906, won by Eben Byers. However, the club was unable to build on its success. Author Daniel Wexler said, 'It had some good bunkering and the green complexes were fairly interesting. There just wasn't any room for it to expand. So inevitably, it would have become a quaint, old relic – even had the Turnpike not been built through it.'

Later, the club was forced to sell off parcels of land to pay its debts. In the mid-1950s it became a favourite hangout for Mafioso and Thomas 'Tommy Ryan' Eboli, a former acting boss of the Genovese crime family, and Joseph 'Joe Bayonne' Zicarelli were club members. In the mid-1960s came the killer blow – the New Jersey Turnpike extension to the nearby George Washington Bridge cut right through the club's property. A housing development now stands on the land where David Hunter made history.

THE ONLY

AMERICAN PRESIDENT
TO CANCEL A POLITICAL MEETING FOR GOLF
William H. Taft, White House, 1600 Pennsylvania Avenue, Washington DC, USA. 1909

A keen golfer despite his huge girth, William Taft used the Schenectady Putter even though it was banned in tournament play. He once cancelled a meeting with the president of Chile to play golf instead. He said, 'I'll be damned if I'll give up my game to see this fellow.'

THE FIRST

PLAYER TO WIN
LADIES' OPEN AMATEUR CHAMPIONSHIP
AND US WOMEN'S AMATEUR CHAMPIONSHIP
IN SAME YEAR

Dorothy Iona Campbell, Ladies' Open Amateur Championship at Birkdale Golf Club, Waterloo Road, Southport, Merseyside, England. 1909; US Women's Amateur Championship at Merion Cricket Club, 325 Montgomery Avenue, Haverford, Pennsylvania, USA. 1909

Dorothy Campbell was born at Edinburgh, Scotland on 24 March 1883 and won the Scottish Ladies' titles in 1905, 1906 and again in 1908. She won the Ladies' Open Amateur Championship for the first time in 1909 beating Florence Hezlet by 4–3. The same year she won the US Amateur title by beating Mrs R. H. Barlow by 3–2. She retained her title the following year beating Mrs G. M. Martin by 2–1.

By August 1924 (she had been Mrs J. B. Hurd for 11 years by now), she became the oldest winner of the US Amateur Championship at 41 years and four months when she defeated former tennis champion Mary Browne by 7–6. In 1911 she won the Ladies' Open Amateur Championship again, this time at Royal Portrush and it was Florence Hezlet's sister Violet who was runner-up – the winning margin was 3–2. She died at Yemassee, South Carolina on 20 March 1945.

THE FIRST

AMERICAN TO WIN
THE US OPEN

JOHN J. MCDERMOTT, CHICAGO GOLF CLUB, WHEATON, ILLINOIS, USA. SATURDAY 24 JUNE 1911

It was the first of his back-to-back US Open titles and McDermott was 19 years, 10 months and 12 days at the time. Born at Philadelphia, Pennsylvania in 1891, Johnny McDermott learned his craft as a caddie and came to prominence when he beat Willie Anderson by one stroke to win the 1910 Philadelphia Open. That same year, he came second in the US Open at the Philadelphia Cricket Club, losing to Alex Smith in a three-way play-off by 71 to 75.

The following year, he was the first American-born player to triumph at the US Open, all the previous 16 winners being British. He not only won (by two shots, also on a three-way play-off 80 to 82 to 85) but also became the youngest player to do so, defeating Mike Brady and George Simpson. On 2 August 1912 he retained his title at the Country Club of Buffalo in New York State.

JOHN MCDERMOTT WAS ALSO: The FIRST teenager to win the US Open in 1911 • The FIRST golfer to break par in the US Open, when he won his second title in 1912

LOSING HIS GRIP

In 1913 Johnny McDermott played in The Open at Hoylake in Britain and finished fifth. The following year he returned to participate but was too late and on his return journey his ship, the *Kaiser Wilhelm II*, collided with the *Incemore* and sank. McDermott spent time in a lifeboat before being rescued. On his return to America he suffered a turn in 1914 at the Atlantic City Golf Club, where he was the professional, and the following year, he had a complete mental breakdown. He never played golf again and spent the rest of his life in lunatic asylums. He died in 1971, six days short of his 80th birthday, still incarcerated.

THE FIRST

PLAYER TO WIN THE OPEN IN THREE DIFFERENT DECADES

HARRY VARDON, THE OPEN AT DUNCUR ROAD, MUIRFIELD, GULLANE, EAST LOTHIAN, SCOTLAND. THURSDAY 11 JUNE 1896; AT PRESTWICK, 2 LINKS ROAD, PRESTWICK, STRATHCLYDE, SCOTLAND. WEDNESDAY 10 JUNE 1903; AT THE ROYAL ST GEORGE'S GOLF CLUB, SANDWICH, KENT, ENGLAND. FRIDAY 30 JUNE 1911

One of the 'Great Triumvirate' along with J. H. Taylor and James Braid, Harry Vardon was the first golfer to win The Open in three separate decades. In 1896 he won the Claret Jug for the first time, scoring 316 (83–78–78–77), the same as J. H. Taylor, but won the play-off by 157 to 161. Remarkably, Vardon at one stage was 11 shots behind the leader. Seven years later, Vardon won The Open again, beating brother Tom by six strokes (300 to 306). Eight years later, Vardon won again and again had to resort to a play-off to beat Frenchman Arnaud Massey after both went round in 303. Massey resigned at the 35th hole to give Vardon his fifth Open title.

Vardon died on 20 March 1937 at his home in Hertfordshire and was buried in St Andrew's parish church, Totteridge, four days later. He was 66. In its obituary *The Times* said:

'He did what only a very great player can do; he raised the general conception of what was possible in his game and forced his nearest rivals to attain a higher standard by attempting that which they would otherwise have deemed impossible.'

Only two other men have ever repeated the feat of winning The Open in three different decades – Vardon's friend and rival and other Triumvirate member J.H. Taylor (1894 at Sandwich, 1900 at St Andrews and 1913 at Hoylake), and more than 60 years later Gary Player (3 July 1959 at Muirfield, 13 July 1968 at Carnoustie and 13 July 1974 at Royal St Lytham).

THE ONLY
BRITON TO WIN
THE US AMATEUR
CHAMPIONSHIP

HAROLD HILTON, US AMATEUR CHAMPIONSHIP AT APAWAMIS CLUB, 2 CLUB ROAD, RYE, NEW YORK, USA. SEPTEMBER 1911

Born at West Kirby, Cheshire in 1869 Harold Horsfall Hilton was a sporting prodigy but excelled at the game of golf. He began playing on the links of The Royal Liverpool Golf Club, Hoylake but retained his amateur status.

Having won the major tournament in England, it seemed fitting that he continue his triumphs overseas. Hilton won the Irish Open Amateur Championship in three consecutive years from 1900 and the Irish Open in 1900 and 1901. Ten years later, he won the Amateur Championship at Prestwick beating E. A. Lassen 4–3.

That same year, Hilton became the first and, to date, only Briton to triumph in the US Amateur Championship. It was the first time the championship went beyond the scheduled 36 holes. Hilton was 6 up with 15 to play on Fred Herreshoff in the final, but the American squared the match after 34 holes. The next two holes were halved to ensure the match went into extra holes. At the 37th hole Hilton played his ball to the right of the green only for it to hit a rock and bounce onto the green. If it had struck the rock at a different angle it could have wrecked his chances of winning. Hilton won by five strokes to four to win the hole and take the title.

Silas Strawn, the president of the USGA, told the crowd that Hilton was the greatest living amateur golfer. Hilton replied that he had been lucky to win. 'I can also testify that your golfers are not lacking in heart. I would also like to correct a statement that has appeared in some of the papers to the effect that I came to this country to win the championship. I did not. I came over to play in it.'

Hilton won his fourth and last amateur championship in 1913 at St Andrews. Hilton was a chain smoker who could get through 50 cigarettes during a round of golf. He was also a prolific author and journalist becoming editor of *Golf Monthly* in 1911, a job he held until 1914. In 1913 he became the editor of *Golf Illustrated* after the death of Gorden Smith. He also wrote, edited or contributed to *The Book of Golf and Golfers* (1899), *Great Golfers: Their Methods at a Glance* (1904), *My Golfing Reminiscences* (1907) and *The Royal and Ancient Game of Golf* (1912). He died of cardiac failure and Parkinson's disease at his home, Bethlehem Westcote, near Kingham, Stow-on-the-Wold, Gloucestershire in 1942 (see 1892, page 55).

THE FIRST

AMATEUR TO WIN
THE US OPEN

Francis Ouimet, Brookline Country Club (original course), 191 Clyde Street, Chestnut Hill, Massachusetts, USA.
Saturday 20 September 1913

At age 20 Francis Ouimet became the first amateur to win the US Open, beating off the challenge of Harry Vardon and Ted Ray in a play-off – he won by 72 to 77 to 78, all three men having scored 304. Ouimet was the son of a coachman and lived across the road from the Brookline Country Club. In 1913 the first qualifying round was played because there were 165 entrants for the competition.

In 1915 Jerome Travers became the second amateur to win and in 1916 another amateur, Chick Evans, won, the only time that amateurs had won the title back-to-back and the third amateur winner in four years. That year was not a good one for Francis Ouimet (1893–1967) who fell foul of the strict laws regarding amateurs and was banned because of his

---

BIOPIC NITPICK

On 30 September 2005 the Walt Disney Organization released a biopic of Francis Ouimet, *The Greatest Game Ever Played*, based on the book by Mark Frost, co-creator with David Lynch of *Twin Peaks*. The film has more than a few factual errors or uses of artistic licence including making the play-off that won the US Open much closer than it actually was. In the film, the contest was decided by an 18th hole putt.

---

involvement with a sporting goods business. The ban was rescinded in 1918 and he won the US Amateur Championship in 1931, 17 years after he first won the title. His redemption was complete in 1951 when he became the first American Captain of the Royal & Ancient Club of St Andrews.

THIS MATCH ALSO INVOLVED: The LAST player to win the US Open at a first attempt

---

THE LAST

OF THE
'GREAT TRIUMVIRATE'
TO WIN THE
OPEN

Harry Vardon, The Open at Prestwick, 2 Links Road, Prestwick, Strathclyde, Scotland. Friday 19 June 1914

One of the Great Triumvirate, Vardon was the last of the trio, which also included J. H. Taylor and James Braid, to win The Open (see also pages 77 and 89). He triumphed at Prestwick in 1914 to win (by three strokes) from Taylor. It was the last Open until 1920 (the First World War intervened, from 1914–1918).

THE FIRST
PLAYER TO WIN
THE US OPEN AND
US AMATEUR CHAMPIONSHIP
IN SAME YEAR

CHICK EVANS: US OPEN AT MINIKAHDA CLUB, 3205 EXCELSIOR
BOULEVARD, MINNEAPOLIS, MINNESOTA, USA. FRIDAY 30 JUNE
1916; US AMATEUR CHAMPIONSHIP AT MERION CRICKET CLUB,
325 MONTGOMERY AVENUE, HAVERFORD, PENNSYLVANIA, USA.
SATURDAY 9 SEPTEMBER 1916

Three months after winning the US Open (the third amateur winner in four years), Charles 'Chick' Evans (1890–1979) won the US Amateur Championship title, the first man to win both titles in the same year. Using just seven hickory-shafted clubs – jigger, mashie, spoon, brassie, lofter, niblick and putter – Evans led the US Open at Minikahda Club, Minnesota from the start with a score of 286 (70–69–74–73) compared to Jock Hutchison's 288 (73–75–72–68). This record that would stand for 20 years. Evans scored 32 on the first nine before finishing with 70.

A little under ten weeks later on 9 September 1916 he triumphed in the US Amateur Championship at Merion, Pennsylvania beating Bob Gardner, the defending champion, by 4 and 3 in the final. Evans had lost the 1912 title to Jerome Travers and had been a semi-finalist on two other occasions so was determined to triumph on this occasion.

The only other golfer in history to win these two tournaments in the same year was Bobby Jones, who did it in 1930, the year of his Grand Slam. Ironically, the 1916 competition was the first that Bobby Jones entered – he was 12 at the time. Evans beat Gardner in front of the biggest crowd to that date to witness a golf competition in the USA. Evans competed in the US Amateur Championship every year from 1907 until 1962, winning again in 1920, beating Francis Ouimet in the final.

Evans was a little eccentric in some of his actions and views. To find a ball in the rough, he would roll around on the floor until he came across the missing ball. He once said:

'I made a rule never to swing a golf club except to hit a golf ball for I had learned that one could swing beautifully when the ball wasn't there and poorly when it was. Most people seem to consider playing as practice and that is one of the reasons that they never emerge from the heap. There is a vast difference between practising golf shots and playing the game of golf.'

Rather than turn professional, in 1916 Evans used the $5,000 prize money to establish a golf scholarship fund for caddies. Since 1930, more than 9,000 Evans Scholars Fund recipients have graduated from colleges. Evans is the only player to have participated in 50 consecutive US Amateur Championships, taking part in his last in 1962, aged 72. On occasion, Evans carried four putters in his bag and chose which one to use depending on the green and its condition. At one stage, he believed that he would never win a title and wrote a piece of doggerel about his efforts:

'I've a semi-final hoodoo, I'm afraid.
I can never do as you do, Jimmy Braid.
I've a genius not to do it,
I excel at almost to it,
But I never can go through it, I'm afraid.'

THE FIRST
US PGA
CHAMPIONSHIP

SIWANOY COUNTRY CLUB, PONDFIELD ROAD, BRONXVILLE, NEW YORK, USA. TUESDAY 10-SATURDAY 14 OCTOBER 1916

The US Professional Golf Association Championship is the oldest and most important of the events that make up the US professional tour. The

THE ONE AND ONLY?

Jim Barnes claimed to have been the only US PGA winner to have won the championship twice. He said, 'That PGA record list is actually in error. I won that 1916 championship at Siwanoy all right but that wasn't the first professional golf championship in the United States. The spring of that year, the New York Newspapermen's Golf Club put on a medal play tournament at Van Courtland Park, which they labelled the Professional Golfers' Championship. They put up a cup. I should know. I have it yet. My winning score was 276.'

winner receives the Wanamaker trophy named for its designer Rodman Wanamaker. It was Wanamaker who on 16 January 1916 hosted the lunch at the Taplow Golf Club in New York City that led to the formation of the Professional Golf Association on 10 April of the same year. He also donated the purse – $2,580 – at the first championship.

Three British-born golfers and a solitary American (Walter Hagen) reached the first semi-finals. Hagen played ex-pat Scot Jack Fowler 'Jock' Hutchison, and looked at one stage as if he would win but Hutchison triumphed 2 up. In the other semi-final, Briton James M. Barnes from Lelant, Cornwall had no problems disposing of Willie MacFarlane, formerly of Aberdeen, Scotland.

In the final Jim Barnes and Jock Hutchison both scored 77 in the first 18 holes. After a meal break, Barnes announced, 'I always do better after lunch.' On the 21st hole he squared the match and took the lead for the first time at the 25th hole with an 18 ft (5.4 metre) putt. On the final green, both players had five-footers for fours and, after a measurement was taken, it was decided that Hutchison was out. Hutchison missed the putt and Barnes made his, winning 1 up to receive $500 and a diamond medal. As runner-up Hutchison received $250 and a gold medal.

In 1919 Barnes won again (there was no US PGA in 1917 or 1918 because of the First World War) and again against a Scottish-born player, Fred McLeod. From 1919 until 1942 and from 1944 until 1957 the competition was a matchplay event.

THE FIRST
AMERICAN GOLFER
TO PLAY 180 HOLES
IN A DAY

EDWARD STYLES, OLD YORK ROAD COUNTRY CLUB, PHILADELPHIA, PENNSYLVANIA, USA. 5.53 AM-8.32 PM FRIDAY 11 JULY 1919

Edward Styles began his marathon day of golf seven minutes before six in the morning one July day after the First World War. He played 10 rounds of golf, consisting of 180 holes and 796 strokes. He played for 13 hours and 10 minutes with an average playing time per round of one hour and 19 minutes. Styles walked for 40 miles (64 km) and took three breaks for food and drink and to change his shoes.

THE ONLY
WOMEN'S GOLF TOURNAMENT
CANCELLED BECAUSE OF A
RAIL STRIKE

The Ladies' British Open Amateur Championship at Burnham and Berrow Golf Club, St Christopher's Way, Burnham-on-Sea, Somerset, England. October 1919

The Ladies' British Open Amateur Championship was not held between 1915 and 1918 because of the First World War and so, after the cessation of hostilities in 1918, the ladies were looking forward to holding their first post-war tournament. It was not to be – the tournament was cancelled due to a national rail strike. Seven years later, the championship was postponed from its original schedule because of the General Strike that crippled Britain in May 1926.

THE LAST

OPEN AT DEAL

**The Open at Royal Cinque Ports Golf Club, Deal, Kent, England.
Wednesday 30 June–Thursday 1 July 1920**

Eleven years after The Open was held at Deal, it was staged there for the second and last time. Only 54 players entered the first Open after the First World War but they included Long Jim Barnes and Walter Hagen on his first trip (he finished last but one). A strong wind made things difficult for the competitors but George Duncan, with the aid of a new driver he had bought at the Championship Exhibition of Golf Equipment, came through victorious with 303 (80–80–71–72) to beat Sandy Herd, the 1902 champion, by two strokes. As well as the Claret Jug, he won £75 and a gold medal.

THE FIRST

WOODEN GOLF TEE

New Jersey, USA. 1921

Twenty-two years after dentist George F. Grant invented the wooden tee, another American dentist William Lowell patented the wooden tee which he called the Reddy Tee, because it was painted red. However, his invention was slow to catch on and despite handing them out gratis, many golfers refused to use them. It was only when he paid Walter Hagen $1,500 to use the red wooden tee that they began to gather wider acceptance.

THE FIRST

INTERNATIONAL
PROFESSIONAL
GOLF CHAMPIONSHIP

GLENEAGLES, SCOTLAND. MONDAY 6 JUNE 1921

Great Britain beat the USA 9–3 in the first international professional championship. The course's designer James Braid, beat Clarence Hackney 5 and 4 in the singles and playing with J. H. Taylor, halved against Hackney and the US Open Champion of 1908, Fred McLeod.

THE FIRST
'AMERICAN'
TO WIN THE OPEN

**Jock Hutchison, The Open at St Andrews, Fife, Scotland.
Saturday 25 June 1921**

The Claret Jug was taken out of Britain for the first time in 1921 when Jack Fowler 'Jock' Hutchison (1884–1977) won it in a 36-hole play-off by nine strokes against Roger Wethered. In the first round Hutchison had scored a hole-in-one on the eighth and almost repeated the feat on the ninth, missing by an inch or two. In the third round Wethered, looking to become the third amateur to win, was penalized a stroke when he stepped on his own ball. Hutchison had been born in Fife but emigrated to the USA, taking citizenship in 1920.

**THIS MATCH ALSO SAW: The ONLY amateur runner-up in
The Open**

THE ONLY

US OPEN

WINNER TO RECEIVE A TROPHY

FROM AN AMERICAN PRESIDENT

JIM BARNES, THE US OPEN AT COLUMBIA COUNTRY CLUB, 7900 CONNECTICUT AVENUE, CHEVY CHASE, MARYLAND, USA. FRIDAY 22 JULY 1921

Jim Barnes stood 6 ft 3 in (1.9 m), which earned him the nickname 'Long Jim'. He won the first US PGA Championship in 1916 and retained the trophy in 1919 when the competition resumed after the First World War. Two years later, he won the US Open beating Fred McLeod and Walter Hagen by nine strokes – 289 to 298. As he approached the 18th hole Barnes was greeted by a US Marines band and presented with his trophy by President Warren Harding. A few days later, Barnes was given lunch at the White House.

THE FIRST

NATIVE-BORN

AMERICAN WINNER

OF THE US

PGA CHAMPIONSHIP

WALTER HAGEN, US PGA AT INWOOD COUNTRY CLUB, 50 PEPPE ROAD, INWOOD, NEW YORK, USA. SATURDAY 1 OCTOBER 1921

The first native-born American to win the US PGA was Walter Hagen in 1921, the fourth time the competition was held. The first three PGAs were won by Britons. In the final Hagen beat Jim Barnes 3 and 2, Barnes having won the first two tournaments in 1916 and 1919.

THE FIRST
US OPEN TO CHARGE AN ADMISSION FEE

THE US OPEN AT SKOKIE COUNTRY CLUB, 500 WASHINGTON AVENUE, GLENCOE, ILLINOIS, USA. MONDAY 15 JULY 1922

On 15 July 1922, twenty-year-old Gene Sarazen, won the first US Open at which spectators were charged an admission fee of $1 to watch the contest. Sarazen finished his fourth round with a birdie for a 68 and a victory by one stroke (over John L. Black). While waiting for the favourites to finish, he quipped, 'I've got mine, let them get theirs.' There were 323 entrants for the competition, which meant that the championship was extended to three days.

THE FIRST
NATIVE-BORN AMERICAN TO WIN THE OPEN

WALTER HAGEN, THE OPEN AT THE ROYAL ST GEORGE'S GOLF CLUB, SANDWICH, KENT, ENGLAND. FRIDAY 23 JUNE 1922

In 1920 Walter Hagen travelled to England to play in The Open for the first time. He was horrified to discover that he was not allowed to enter the clubhouse at Deal, so he hired a Daimler which his chauffeur parked ostentatiously in front of the main entrance and Hagen not so subtly changed in full view of anyone who happened to be passing. He also hired a butler who met him every day on the 18th hole with a refreshing drink on a tray.

Two years later, Hagen returned to England for The Open at Sandwich. Hagen trailed the defending champion Jock Hutchison at the start of the final round by two strokes but returned a 72. It was the first of his four wins in all (1922, 1924, 1928, 1929). On the night before the first round Hagen was still propping up the bar at 2 am. When he was told that all his opponents were probably in bed, he replied, 'Maybe they're in bed but they're not sleeping.'

—•◆•—

THE FIRST
PLAYER TO WIN THE US OPEN AND US PGA CHAMPIONSHIP IN THE SAME YEAR

GENE SARAZEN AT THE US OPEN AT SKOKIE COUNTRY CLUB, 500 WASHINGTON AVENUE, GLENCOE, ILLINOIS, USA. MONDAY 15 JULY 1922; US PGA CHAMPIONSHIP AT OAKMONT COUNTRY CLUB, 1233 HULTON ROAD, OAKMONT, PENNSYLVANIA, USA. FRIDAY 18 AUGUST 1922

Having won the US Open in July 1922 with a score of 288 for 72 holes, 20-year-old Gene Sarazen won the US PGA title the following month becoming the youngest winner. He beat his great rival Emmet French 4–3 in the final. Sarazen received a purse of $500 and a diamond medal.

THE FIRST

WALKER CUP

NATIONAL GOLF LINKS OF AMERICA, SEBONAC INLET ROAD, SOUTHAMPTON, LONG ISLAND, NEW YORK, USA.

MONDAY 28–TUESDAY 29 AUGUST 1922

The Walker Cup for the leading amateur golfers of the USA, Great Britain and Ireland is named for George Herbert Walker, the grandfather of President George Bush and great-grandfather of President George W. Bush, who was president of the US Golf Association in 1920. That year he visited St Andrews to discuss a competition and on his return offered a plan for an International Challenge Trophy – the newspapers picked up on the story and labelled it the Walker Cup.

An unofficial event was held in 1921 after the US Golf Association invited all countries to send teams to compete but none accepted. William Fownes Jr. organized an informal team (Charles Evans Jr., Jesse Guilford, Paul Hunter, Bobby Jones, Francis Ouimet, J. Wood Platt, Frederick J. Wright Jr. and Fownes himself) that he took to Hoylake. There they defeated a British team (Tommy Armour, C. C. Aylmer, Ernest Holderness, J. L. C. Jenkins, R. H. de Montmorency, J. Gordon Simpson, Cyril Tolley and Roger Wethered) by 9 to 3 on the day before the amateur championships.

The competition proper began in 1922 when the Royal & Ancient sent a team to America towards the end of the summer. Covering that competition was journalist Bernard Darwin of *The Times* who found himself playing when the British captain Robert Harris became incapacitated. Darwin proved himself one of the few journalists who could walk the walk as well as talking the talk when he won his singles match. Darwin had an excellent pedigree – he was the grandson of Charles Darwin, he practised law on leaving Cambridge but decided to concentrate on writing about golf instead. He was also twice a Semi-Finalist in the Amateur championship.

There was a further tournament in 1923 at St Andrews and 1924 at Garden City Golf Club, New York when it became biennial. In 1926 the

American team was beaten 6–3 in a foursome challenge match by the Moles Golfing Society at Woking, Surrey. Bobby Jones captained the American side while Robert Harris, the Amateur Champion, led the Moles. After the Second World War the tournament was held in odd-numbered years. The British amateurs did not score their first victory over the USA until 1938 at St Andrews. Indeed, in 1936 they failed to win a single match.

THE FIRST
PLAYER TO WIN THE US OPEN IN SPECTACLES

Willie Macfarlane, US Open at Worcester Country Club, 2 Rice Street, Worcester, Massachusetts, USA. Friday 5 June 1925

Willie Macfarlane (1890–1961) saw off a challenge from Bobby Jones to win the 1925 US Open but it took him two play-offs to do so. Both men had played the four rounds in 291 strokes, Macfarlane's second round of seven being a new low. In the play-off Macfarlane took 147 strokes while Jones took one more. It would not be until 1974 that another bespectacled player won the US Open when Hale Irwin triumphed in the championship. Irwin also won in 1979 and 1990.

THE LAST
OPEN AT PRESTWICK

THE OPEN AT 2 LINKS ROAD, PRESTWICK, STRATHCLYDE, SCOTLAND. THURSDAY 25–FRIDAY 26 JUNE 1925

Sixty-five years after it hosted the first Open, the 24th and last tournament was held at Prestwick and the Claret Jug was won by Jim Barnes (1897–1966) of America who carded 300. The competition had only been held four times in the 20th century at Prestwick. The course is hampered by difficult terrain (the Pow Burn runs through the course), plus too many spectators (10,000 attended the last tournament) and too few stewards have meant that The Open has been staged elsewhere ever since.

THE ONLY
PLAYER TO WIN THE
BRITISH PGA MATCHPLAY
CHAMPIONSHIP WITH
THREE CADDIES

ARCHIE COMPSTON, BRITISH PGA MATCHPLAY CHAMPIONSHIP AT MOOR PARK GOLF CLUB, RICKMANSWORTH, HERTFORDSHIRE, ENGLAND. 1925

Archie Compston was born at Wolverhampton, Staffordshire in 1894 and was a highly successful if eccentric golfer during the 1920s. He won the British PGA Matchplay Championship in 1925 and 1927 and was the only player to require the services of three caddies. The first carried his clubs, the second his clothes in case he felt a change was necessary and the third was responsible for his cigarettes, cigars and pipes as he chain-smoked his way around the course. He died on 8 August 1962.

THE FIRST
TOURNAMENT TO OFFER A
FIVE-FIGURE PURSE

Los Angeles Open, Los Angeles Country Club, 10101 Wilshire Boulevard, Los Angeles, Los Angeles, California, USA. February 1926

The Los Angeles Open, the third-oldest surviving PGA Tour event, began in 1926. It was also the first tournament to offer a $10,000 purse.

Harry Cooper won the first event beating George Von Elm by three strokes. The writer Damon Runyon nicknamed Cooper 'Lighthorse' because of the speed of his play. Cooper picked up a cheque for $3,500 for his win.

The tournament has undergone a number of name changes over the years, usually because of different sponsors. From 1926 until 1970 it was the Los Angeles Open, then from 1971 until 1983 it was the Glen Campbell Los Angeles Open. In 1984, 1985 and 1986 it was once again the Los Angeles Open. In 1987 and 1988 it was the Los Angeles Open Presented by Nissan. From 1989 until 1994 it was the Nissan Los Angeles Open. From 1995 until 2007 it was the Nissan Open. On 15 October 2007 Chicago-based Northern Trust Corporation agreed a five-year deal and it became the Northern Trust Open.

Since 7 January 1973 the tournament has been staged almost exclusively at the Riviera Country Club. In 1983 it was held at Rancho Park Golf Course and in 1998 at Valencia Country Club in Valencia, California. The competition has also had a peripatetic existence. After the first year at the Los Angeles Country Club, it moved to El Caballero Country Club in Tarzana, California in 1927 and the following year to Wilshire Country Club, also in LA. In 1929 (the year it became the first golf tournament broadcast on the wireless) and 1930 it was held at the Riviera Country Club in Pacific Palisades. In 1931 and 1933 it was hosted at the Wilshire Country Club and in 1932 at the Hillcrest Country Club. From 1934 until 1936 the Los Angeles Open was played at Los Angeles Country Club. In 1937, 1938 and 1939 it was played at Griffith Park and again at Los Angeles Country Club in 1940. The following year it was played again at the Riviera Country Club in Pacific Palisades and again at Hillcrest Country Club in 1941 before America entered the Second World War. It was at Wilshire Country Club that the event began again in 1944. From 1945 until 1953 it was held at the Riviera Country Club in Pacific Palisades. In 1954 the tournament was played at Fox Hills Country Club on land that is now in Culver City, California and in 1955 it moved to Inglewood Country Club in Inglewood, California. From 1956 until 9 January 1972 it was played at Rancho Park Golf Course, Los Angeles with the exception of 1968 when the event was played at Brookside Golf Course in Pasadena, California.

There has been a huge jump in prize money since the first prize of $3,500 offered in 1926, to the modern era when Rory Sabbatini won the 80th anniversary Nissan Open with a prize of $918,000.

THE FIRST

PLAYER TO DO THE DOUBLE

Bobby Jones, The Open at Royal Lytham & St Annes Golf Club, Links Gate, Lytham St Annes, Lancashire, England. Thursday 24 June 1926; US Open at Scioto Country Club, 2196 Riverside Drive, Columbus, Ohio, USA. Saturday 10 July 1926

Robert Tyre Jones was born on 17 March 1902 and was such a sickly child that he was five before he was able to eat solid food. At six, he took up golf and the game fortified him and by 14 he had made it to the third round in the 1916 US Amateur Championship. He was the youngest player in the competition and his immaturity perhaps led him to situations where he was unable to control his emotions. One sportswriter said that Jones had 'the face of an angel and the temper of a timber wolf'.

In 1923 he won the first of his 13 Majors and his first US Open. Jones would go on to win his titles in just 20 attempts.

Three years later 'in 1926' Jones became the first player and, to date, only amateur to do the Double, winning The Open and the US Open. Jones won the Claret Jug (in its first year at Royal Lytham) by two strokes 291 (72–72–73–74) to Al Watrous's 293 (71–75–69–78). Jones was lucky to win – he left his identity badge at the hotel and despite being internationally known, the steward on the gate refused to let him on to the course without identification. Without the time to go back to the hotel and having overcome the temper tantrums that plagued much of his early career, Jones calmly bought an admission ticket that cost him 2s 6d and went on to win, becoming the first player who had to pay a spectator's fee to play.

At the US Open, which was extended to three days again and had a record entry of 694 players Jones beat Joe Turnesa by one stroke – 293 (70–79–71–73) to 294 (71–74–72–77). Bobby Jones died in 1971.

THIS PLAYER WAS ALSO: The ONLY amateur to do the Double

THE FIRST

OFFICIAL
NATIONAL COMPETITION
FOR BLACK GOLFERS

THE NATIONAL COLORED GOLF CHAMPIONSHIP AT MAPLEDALE COUNTRY CLUB, STOW, MASSACHUSETTS, USA. SATURDAY 4-SUNDAY 5 SEPTEMBER 1926

In the summer of 1925 a group of black golfers founded The United States Colored Golfers Association and held the first competition over the Fourth of July weekend at the Shady Rest Golf Club, Westfield, New Jersey. Harry Jackson won the $25 first prize by beating Harry Shippen by three shots.

The following year the first official national competition was held for black golfers at Stow, Massachusetts. It was a two-day, 72-hole tournament. The first three National Colored Golf championships were held at Mapledale, but in 1929 it closed and the National, as it came to be called, moved around America. That same year the United States Colored Golfers Association changed its name to the United Golfers Association. The competition was not restricted to black players. Chairman Norris Horton said, 'We knew what it was like to be excluded and we didn't want to do the same to anybody else, so blacks, whites, anybody who qualified and paid the entry free could play.'

THE FIRST

RYDER CUP

**WORCESTER COUNTRY CLUB, 2 RICE STREET, WORCESTER,
MASSACHUSETTS, USA. FRIDAY 3–SATURDAY 4 JUNE 1927**

The Ryder Cup was contested between Britain and America until September 1979 when America's opponents became Europe. The gold cup was commissioned in 1926 but was not ready for the unofficial match played that year. The cup stands 17 in (43 cm) high and weighs just 4 lb (1.8 kg). The player on the top of the trophy is a representation of Abe Mitchell, who was a friend and golf teacher (at a cost of £1,000 a year) to seed merchant Samuel Ryder as well as a gardener. In 1927 a bout of appendicitis prevented his participation in the first Ryder Cup, but Mitchell played for Britain in 1929, 1931 and 1933. The cup was donated by Ryder who also offered each player on the winning team £5.

The competition proper began following an exhibition match in 1926 between British golfers from the East Course, Wentworth Club, Virginia Water, Surrey and a similar American team. The British won 13½ to 1½. In the first competition proper Britain captained by Ted Ray took to the links opposite an American team captained by Walter Hagen. Ray was the oldest competitor on the Ryder Cup being 50 years, 2 months and 5 days old. The Americans won easily by 9½ to 2½, winning three of the four 36-hole foursomes and six of the single matches. George Duncan won the solitary single for Britain against Joe Turnesa.

Europe would not beat the Americans on their home soil until 27 September 1987 when they defeated a team, captained by Jack Nicklaus, at the Muirfield Village course, which the Golden Bear designed. The usually friendly rivalry between the two teams was put to the test in September 1999 when the competition was held at Brookline, Massachusetts. The singles matches ended with Justin Leonard holing a lengthy putt in his match with José María Olazábal. Several of the American players and their wives ran across the green to congratulate Leonard and some ran across Olazábal's line, seeming to forget that the Spaniard still had a putt to win and to treat him with less than respect. In the end, Olazábal missed his putt but several of

---

SEED CAPTAIN

Samuel Ryder was the first person to sell seeds in the little packets we know today. He did not begin playing golf until he was 50 but took to the game with a passion, practising six days a week at his home, Marlborough House, in Surrey. In 1911 he became captain of the Verulam Golf Club in St Albans and was also captain in 1926 and 1927.

---

the European team were annoyed at what they saw as a distinct lack of sporting behaviour from the American side.

THE ONLY
ONE-EYED
PLAYER TO WIN
THE US OPEN

TOMMY ARMOUR, US OPEN AT OAKMONT COUNTRY CLUB, 1233 HULTON ROAD, OAKMONT, PENNSYLVANIA, USA. FRIDAY 17 JUNE 1927

Born at 18 Balcarres Street, Edinburgh on 24 September 1896 (the same day as F. Scott Fitzgerald), Thomas Dickson Armour enlisted with the Black Watch at the outbreak of the First World War after graduating from the University of Edinburgh. In 1918, having gained a reputation as a machine-gunner, he transferred to the recently established tank corps but was injured during a German attack of mustard gas and lost the sight of his left eye.

On the cessation of hostilities, he returned to the golf course but was much slower when it came to lining up shots, replying to critics 'Whoever said golf was supposed to be played fast?' In 1919, as an amateur, he finished second in the Irish Open and in 1920 he won the French Amateur

Championship. In 1922 after playing for Scotland against England, he took American citizenship and became secretary of the Westchester-Biltmore Club based in New York, where he was reportedly paid $10,000 a year. In 1924 he became a professional and three years later beat Harry Cooper in a play-off by 76 to 79, holing a 10 ft (3 metre) birdie putt on the 72nd green to win the US Open at Oakmont. The two men had tied on 301 with Armour scoring 78–71–76–76 (see 1953, page 145).

THE ONLY
PLAYER TO WIN
THE US PGA
FOUR YEARS IN A ROW

WALTER HAGEN. FRENCH LICK SPRINGS, 8670 WEST STATE ROAD 56, FRENCH LICK, INDIANA, USA. SATURDAY 20 SEPTEMBER 1924; OLYMPIA FIELDS COUNTRY CLUB, 2800 COUNTRY CLUB DRIVE, OLYMPIA FIELDS, ILLINOIS, USA. SATURDAY 26 SEPTEMBER 1925; SALISBURY GOLF LINKS, WESTBURY, LONG ISLAND, NEW YORK, USA. SATURDAY 25 SEPTEMBER 1926; CEDAR CREST COUNTRY CLUB, 1800 SOUTHERLAND AVENUE, DALLAS, TEXAS, USA. SATURDAY 5 NOVEMBER 1927

Flamboyant Walter Charles Hagen (born the son of a blacksmith in 1892) won the US Open twice (in 1914 and in 1919, having been up all night drinking with his close friend Al Jolson, he went straight to the first tee from a party). In 1922 he became the first native-born American to win the Claret Jug at The Open, which he went on to win four times in all (1922, 1924, 1928, 1929). He captained the American Ryder Cup team six times and won the US PGA Championship a record-tying five times, but remains the only player to win it four years in a row.

On his way to his second title, Hagen beat Tom Harmon 6 and 5 in the first round, saw off the challenge of Al Watrous by 4 and 3 in the second round and beat Johnny Farrell 3 and 2 in the quarter-finals. In the semi-final he was drawn against Ray Derr and won by 8 and 7. In the final he met Jim Barnes who had defeated Larry Nabholtz. However, a faulty putter belonging to Barnes resulted in Hagen's victory. He lost a hole four times in a morning session but in the afternoon on the front nine holes scored 34 and hit a birdie on the 29th hole to pull Hagen's lead back to 1 up. The 30th and 31st holes were shared one each and then Hagen went on to win the 34th hole but took three putts on the 35th, his second one missing from just three feet. On the last hole Barnes needed a win to tie but a poorly executed drive followed by a shanked mashie niblick gave the title to Hagen, 2 up.

The following year, in the first round Hagen beat Al Watrous 1 up but it took him 39 holes to do so. Watrous had led for much of the match. In the second round Hagen beat Mike Brady 7 and 6, and in the quarter final he almost blew it against Leo Diegel as it took him five holes to make par. With the front nine decided, Diegel led 4 up and finished the round 5 up. Hagen played well to cut the deficit to 2 down after the 27th hole, but both players went halves on the next five holes. The match went into extra time and Hagen finally won 1 up on the 40th hole. In the semi-final he beat Harry Cooper 3 and 1. Hagen eagled the first hole of his final match against Bill Mehlhorn and went on to a 6 and 5 victory by the 31st hole.

In the first 18 holes of the deciding match, Hagen and Mehlhorn both went out in 33, with Hagen clinging to a 1 up lead. In the afternoon session Hagen played brilliantly and Mehlhorn was never really in the game.

In September 1926, Hagen won his fourth PGA Championship in six years with a 5 and 3 victory in the final over Leo Diegel. Hagen's opponent was suffering from nerves. On the first hole in the afternoon he drove one ball too far and it ended under a car on a road. When the owner moved the vehicle, Diegel's found his ball in a deep rut. It took him three attempts to get it on the green, and he lost the hole to go 3 down. After 27 holes, Hagen led by two but won the 28th and 31st holes to go 4 up. On the 33rd hole Diegel hit a six to give Hagen his fourth PGA Championship. On his way Hagen had beaten Joe Turnesa 3 and 2 in the first round, Dick Grout 7 and 6 in the second round, Pat Doyle 6 and 5 in the quarter-finals and Johnny Farrell 6 and 5 in the semi-final.

Hagen's fourth and final consecutive win came at Cedar Crest Country Club in Dallas, Texas on 5th November 1927. On the way he had dispatched Jack Farrell 3 and 2 in the first round. In the second round he saw off the challenge of Tony Manero 11 and 10 and Tommy Armour (the reigning US Open Champion) 4 and 3 in the quarter-finals. In the semi-final he beat Al Espinosa 1 up. However, the match was closely fought and Espinosa won the 35th hole to go 1 up. On the second shot to the final green, Espinosa was 25 ft (7.6 metres) away, with Hagen over the green. Pundits, the crowd and the other competitors were convinced that Hagen was going to lose, because he had no chance to make the birdie he needed. However, Hagen was not the defending champion for nothing and he hit a great chip shot to get four. Espinosa needed two putts for the victory. The yips got him and left his approach putt a yard short. He then missed what should have been the match-winning putt.

The players began a play-off and, on the first hole, Espinosa again repeated his three-putt, and Hagen won the match to meet Joe Turnesa in the final. On the first round in the morning Turnesa shot 71 compared to Hagen's 77 but went to lunch with only a 2 up lead. As with the year before, Hagen's opponent began suffering from nerves, and putts that he had sank with ease in the early rounds became difficult to get into the cup. On the final six holes, the yips became even worse and Turnesa missed easy putt after easy putt. Hegan birdied on the 29th hole to square the match and took a 1 up lead when Turnesa bogeyed at the 31st hole. Turnesa left a putt short on the lip on the final hole that would have forced a play-off to give Hagen the title.

Walter Hagen would not win the US PGA Championship again – the best he would achieve would be to tie in third place in 1929. He played for the last time in the tournament in 1935 when he tied in 35th place but his place in golfing history was already assured. The doyen of golf commentators Peter Alliss described Hagen as 'one of the greatest golfers of all time ... [and] has a strong claim indeed to be considered the best matchplayer ever.' He summed up his philosophy to life with the words, 'I never wanted to be a millionaire. I just wanted to live like one. Don't hurry, don't worry, you're only here for a short visit so be sure to smell the flowers along the way.' Hagen died on 6 October 1969 at Traverse City, Michigan, and Arnold Palmer was one of his pallbearers.

THE FIRST

MINIATURE GOLF COURSE

LOOKOUT MOUNTAIN, NEAR CHATTANOOGA, TENNESSEE, USA. 1927

The first miniature golf course was laid out on the summit of Lookout Mountain. It was an 18-hole course complete with doglegs, sand traps and water hazards and was the brainchild of hotelier John Garnet Carter, who patented the name Tom Thumb, the name of a midget golf system. However, some doubt remains as to whether Lookout Mountain was the first miniature course since some sources list a course in Pinehurst, North Carolina that opened eleven years before in 1916.

THE FIRST

WINNER OF AERIAL GOLF

WILLIE HAMMOND, THE WESTBURY GOLF CLUB, 270 WHEATLEY ROAD, OLD WESTBURY, NEW YORK, USA. SUNDAY 27 MAY 1928

Always on the lookout for a new form of the game, in 1928 a team led by Willie Hammond became the first winner of aerial golf. Players boarded an aeroplane and then dropped their balls wrapped in cloth so that they did not bounce over the green. Those balls that landed nearest the cup won the hole. Hammond's team won by three holes. In 1931 RAF Captain Pennington challenged the local pro at Sonning, Reading to a match of aerial golf. Pennington took 80 balls up with him and dropped them through his bomb sight. The club pro played the game in the usual way. He took 68 shots while Pennington took just 29.

THE FIRST
WINNER OF THE REPLICA
CLARET JUG

WALTER HAGEN, THE OPEN AT THE ROYAL ST GEORGE'S GOLF CLUB, SANDWICH, KENT, ENGLAND. FRIDAY 11 MAY 1928

In 1927 Bobby Jones became the last winner of The Open presented with the Claret Jug. Afterwards, the organizing committee of the championship decided to keep the trophy permanently and commissioned a replica to be presented to the winner of The Open. The first recipient of the replica was Walter Hagen who beat Gene Sarazen by two strokes (292 to 294). The original trophy is on display in the clubhouse of the Royal & Ancient Golf Club at St Andrews alongside the Challenge Belt that was the first prize and won permanently by Young Tom Morris (see page 45).

THE FIRST
BLACK MEMBER OF THE
PROFESSIONAL GOLFERS'
ASSOCIATION OF AMERICA

Dewey Brown, USA. 1928.

In 1928 Dewey Brown became the first known black member of the Professional Golfers' Association of America at a time when only white people could belong. He was celebrated for his work as a club-maker and teacher and even made a set of clubs for President Warren G. Harding. Six years after he was made a member, he was stripped of his membership when it came to light that Brown was not in fact white as the committee had thought but actually black, albeit very light-skinned. Brown worked as the assistant golf pro at Shawnee in Pennsylvania and in 1947 he bought Cedar River Golf Club in Indian Lake, New York. His son took over the running of the business when Mr Brown retired in 1972.

THE LAST

MAJOR TOURNAMENT WIN BY WALTER HAGEN

THE OPEN AT DUNCUR ROAD, MUIRFIELD, GULLANE, EAST LOTHIAN, SCOTLAND. FRIDAY 10 MAY 1929

In 1929 Hagen won for the fourth and final time at The Open, his first victory coming in 1922. In 1929 Hagen never took more than five at any hole and won by six strokes. He was presented with the trophy by the Prince of Wales (later Edward VIII, then the Duke of Windsor after his abdication).

THE LAST

AMATEUR TO WIN THE OPEN

BOBBY JONES AT THE ROYAL LIVERPOOL GOLF CLUB, 30 MEOLS DRIVE, HOYLAKE, WIRRAL, ENGLAND. FRIDAY 20 JUNE 1930

Golfing legend Bobby Jones won The Open in 1930, the last amateur to win the Claret Jug. He won by two strokes over Mexican Leo Diegel and American Macdonald Smith. His winning score was 70–72–74–75 for a total of 291.

THE FIRST

W.C. FIELDS SOUND FILM

THE GOLF SPECIALIST, RKO, HOLLYWOOD, CALIFORNIA, USA. RELEASED FRIDAY 22 AUGUST 1930

The first sound film made by the curmudgeonly comedian was *The Golf Specialist*, in which he played J. Effingham Bellweather who while staying at a Florida hotel plays a round with the house detective's flirty wife and a useless caddie. Fields was a keen golfer and indeed bought a house next to a golf course. Living up to his reputation as a curmudgeon, he took against the geese that often landed in his back garden. He would chase them away with a club shouting, 'Either sh*t green or get off my lawn.'

THE ONLY
SPORTSMAN TO RECEIVE TWO TICKER-TAPE PARADES IN NEW YORK

BOBBY JONES, NEW YORK, NEW YORK, USA. FRIDAY 2 JULY 1926 AND WEDNESDAY 2 JULY 1930

The first ever ticker-tape parade was a spontaneous event on 29 October 1886 during the dedication for the Statue of Liberty, and the first for sporting figures was on 6 August 1924 for the American Olympic team. Jones was the first individual sportsman to receive such an accolade (beating the swimmer Gertrude Ederle by almost two months) on 2 July 1926. Jones is, to date, the only sporting personality honoured with two ticker-tape parades in the Big Apple.

THE ONLY
PLAYER TO WIN THE GRAND SLAM

BOBBY JONES, AMATEUR CHAMPIONSHIP AT OLD COURSE AT ST ANDREWS, FIFE, SCOTLAND. SATURDAY 31 MAY 1930; THE OPEN AT ROYAL LIVERPOOL GOLF CLUB, 30 MEOLS DRIVE, HOYLAKE, WIRRAL, ENGLAND. FRIDAY 20 JUNE 1930; US OPEN AT INTERLACHEN GOLF CLUB, 6200 INTERLACHEN BOULEVARD, EDINA, MINNEAPOLIS, USA. SATURDAY 20 JULY 1930; US AMATEUR CHAMPIONSHIP AT MERION CRICKET CLUB, 325 MONTGOMERY AVENUE, HAVERFORD, PENNSYLVANIA, USA. SATURDAY 27 SEPTEMBER 1930

In 1930 Jones won The Open, the US Open, the British and US Amateur championships. On 31 May 1930 he won the Amateur Championship at St Andrews by 7 and 6 over Roger Wethered. On 20 June 1930 he won

The Open at The Royal Liverpool Golf Club, Hoylake, Cheshire. On 12 July 1930 he won the US Open at Interlachen Golf Club, Minneapolis by two strokes over Macdonald Smith (287 to 298).

He completed his Grand Slam – or Impregnable Quadrilateral – on 27 September 1930 on the East Course at Merion Cricket Club, beating Eugene V. Homans by 8 and 7. His third round of 68 was then the lowest in the US Open, and total of 287 was only the third time that par had been broken every fourth round. There were 1,177 entrants and the 1930 US Open was the last in which the 1.62 in (41 mm) ball was used.

Jones was consistent in his US Opens – in his last nine he won four and was second four times. From 1923 until 1930 he was victorious in either the US Open or US Amateur championships but until 1930, he never won both. Professional Bobby Cruickshank bet on Jones to win the Grand Slam at odds of 120–1 and won $60,000. Jones decided to retire from the sport at the young age of 28 and practise law full-time. He said, '[Championships are] something like a cage. First, you are expected to get into it and then you are expected to stay there. But of course, nobody can stay there.'

THE FIRST

PLAYER TO WIN THE US OPEN WITH STEEL-SHAFTED CLUBS

BILLY BURKE, THE US OPEN AT INVERNESS CLUB, 4601 DORR STREET, TOLEDO, OHIO, USA. MONDAY 6 JULY 1931

Billy Burke, a former iron worker, became the first player to win the US Open using steel-shafted clubs. All the previous winners had used clubs manufactured with wooden shafts. Burke won the longest championship on record as it took a 72-hole play-off (two sets of 36) to separate him from runner-up George von Elm. They had tied on 292, then again on 149 before Burke triumphed 148 to 149.

THE FIRST

FILM PLAGIARISM SUIT SETTLED ON A GOLF COURSE

Howard Hughes vs Howard Hawks, Lakeside Country Club, 4500 West Lakeside Drive, Burbank, California, USA. 1931

In July 1930 billionaire industrialist and film producer Howard Hughes issued a writ against director Howard Hawks claiming that sections of *Dawn Patrol* (1930), directed by Hawks, had been copied from Hughes's film *Hell's Angels* (premièred 30 June 1930). One day as Hawks prepared to tee off at the Lakeside Country Club near Universal Studios, the club pro told him that Howard Hughes was on the phone and wanted to play a round with him. Hawks told the pro to tell Hughes he did not want to play golf with him. The pro returned with a message that Hughes would drop the lawsuit if Hawks agreed to play golf. Hawks agreed and beat Hughes. By the time they had played 18 holes, Hawks had agreed to make *Scarface* (released March 1932) for Hughes.

THE ONLY

US WOMEN'S OPEN WINNER TO WIN TWO OLYMPIC GOLD MEDALS

BABE DIDRIKSON, LOS ANGELES, USA. SUNDAY 31 JULY 1932 (JAVELIN); THURSDAY 4 AUGUST 1932 (HURDLES)

Sixteen years before she won the US Women's Open, Mildred 'Babe' Didrikson (later Mrs George Zaharias) won gold medals for javelin and

80 metre hurdles at the Los Angeles Olympics. In both competitions she broke the existing records – 143 ft 4 in (43.6 metres) for the javelin (with her first throw) and 11.7 seconds for the hurdles. In the hurdles heat she equalled the world record of 11.8 seconds before beating it in the final.

She was also a more than useful billiards player, and at Jersey City on 25 July 1931 set a world record for throwing a baseball – 98 yd, 2ft (90 metres). On 4 July 1932 Didrikson took part in the American Athletics Union Olympic trials on the campus of Northwestern University at Evanston, Illinois. Didrikson was the entire team for the Employers Casualty Insurance Company of Dallas. Over the course of three hours, Didrikson took part in eight of the ten events and won six of them. She set world records for the javelin, 80-metre hurdles and the high jump. She also won the shot put, the long jump and baseball throw and was fourth in the discus. When the points were added up, the emcee announced that winner of the team competition was Babe Didrikson with 30 points. In second place with 22 points was the University of Illinois who had sent 22 athletes to participate.

Although Didrikson had qualified for five Olympic events she was to compete in only three so she chose the three in which she had set world records. On the way to the Games, she irritated her fellow competitors by bragging about her achievements, but while her braggadocio annoyed the other athletes it delighted journalists who realized that she gave great copy.

THE FIRST

CURTIS CUP
MATCH

WENTWORTH GOLF CLUB, WENTWORTH DRIVE, VIRGINIA WATER, SURREY, ENGLAND. 1932

The Curtis Cup had its origins at Cromer, Norfolk when the Curtis sisters – Harriot (1881–1974; winner of the US Women's Amateur Golf Championship in 1906 and runner-up in 1907) and Margaret (1883–1965; who had won it in 1907, 1911 and 1912) – played an informal international match against American players at the 1905 Ladies' British Open Amateur Championship. It took almost 30 years for the first tournament featuring the cup that bears their name to come into being. The sisters donated it in 1927 but it was not until 1931 that the USGA agreed to finance an American team while the responsibility for the Great Britain & Ireland team fell to the Ladies' Golf Union.

The first match was held at Wentworth with the British team captained by Joyce Wethered (the only time she participated) and included Wanda Morgan, Enid Wilson, Molly Gourlay, Doris Park, Diana Fishwick, Elsie Corlett and Mrs J.B. Watson. The Americans led by Marion Hollins consisted of Mrs Edwin H. Vare (aka Glenna Collett-Vare), Maureen Orcutt, Virginia Van Wie, Opal Hill, Helen Hicks, Leona Pressler Cheney and Dorothy Higbie. The Americans won by 5 to 3.

The first Curtis Cup Match held at St Andrews did not take place until 2008 and was won by the USA. The silver bowl, designed by Paul Revere, bears the legend, 'To stimulate friendly rivalry among the women golfers of many lands.' In 1984 the Match was played at Muirfield but ladies were not allowed to enter the clubhouse. Finally, the competitors were given a brief tour of the clubhouse and a notice was pinned up apologizing to the male members for any inconvenience that this might cause.

THE LAST
AMATEUR TO WIN THE US OPEN

JOHNNY GOODMAN, AT NORTH SHORE GOLF CLUB, 1340 GLENVIEW ROAD, GLENVIEW, ILLINOIS, USA. SATURDAY 10 JUNE 1933

Johnny Goodman (1910–1970) became the fifth and to date last amateur to win the US Open. He won by just one stroke over Ralph Guldahl – 287 to 288. Goodman scored 75–66–70–76. Goodman came from a poor background and when he was 14 his mother died after giving birth to her 13th child. He travelled to the 1929 US Amateur Championship in Pebble Beach in a cattle truck. Goodman is also one of only five players to win the US Open and the US Amateur Championship, a title he won in 1937. Goodman did not turn professional until 1960, supporting himself as an insurance salesman.

THE ONLY
RYDER CUP CAPTAIN
WHO NEVER PLAYED
IN THE COMPETITION

J. H. Taylor, Great Britain vs USA at Southport and Ainsdale Golf Club, Bradshaws Lane, Ainsdale, Southport, Merseyside, England. Monday 26–Tuesday 27 June 1933

In 1933, J. H. Taylor, five times winner of the Claret Jug at The Open and then aged 62, became the only Ryder Cup captain who never played in the matches. The competition, the fourth to be held, was won by Great Britain by 6 to 5 points. Walter Hagen had captained the first six American Ryder Cup teams (1927, 1929, 1931, 1933, 1935 and 1937).

THE FIRST
CORPORATE
SPONSOR

HERSHEY CHOCOLATE CORPORATION, HERSHEY OPEN AT WEST COURSE, HERSHEY COUNTRY CLUB, 1000 EAST DERRY ROAD, HERSHEY, PENNSYLVANIA, USA. FRIDAY 1–SATURDAY 2 SEPTEMBER 1933

The Hershey Country Club West Course was designed by Maurice McCarthy, the noted golf-course designer who also designed Hershey's public course, the Hershey Parkview Golf Course. The course was expected to be better than the National Golf Links of America in Southampton,

New York so that it could hold prestigious events such as the US Open. In 1930 the first floor of Milton Hershey's home, High Point, became the clubhouse for the new country club.

In 1933 the US Professional Golfers Association suggested that the Hershey Club host a tournament and the result was the first corporate-sponsored competition – this was the Hershey Open, which was part of the US PGA Tour from 1933 to 1939 and again in 1941. (There was no tournament in 1940 because between 26 August and 1 September of that year the Hershey Country Club hosted the PGA Championship, which was won by Byron Nelson.) The first winner of the Hershey Open was Ed Dudley and the last was Ben Hogan who succeeded Henry Picard as the Hershey Club pro on 27 April 1941 (and worked there until 15 June 1951). Picard had won the Hershey Open in 1936 and 1937.

THE FIRST
US MASTERS

US MASTERS AT AUGUSTA NATIONAL GOLF CLUB, 2604 WASHINGTON ROAD, AUGUSTA, GEORGIA, USA. THURSDAY 22 MARCH 1934

The US Masters was founded by golfing legend Bobby Jones and Clifford Roberts. The course is based on the first great nursery of the south which was created by the Belgian horticulturist Baron Berckmans. The tournament was not at first called the Masters because founder Jones thought it too presumptuous. The original name was the Augusta National Invitation Tournament and it stayed that way for five years until Jones relented and the name was officially changed.

Although he retired in 1930, Jones played in the first US Masters because they were short of a big name to draw the crowds and because the club needed the money. Jones finished in joint 13th place. The first US Masters was won on 25 March 1934 by Horton Smith of the USA by one shot over Craig Woods, also an American. The present-day back and front nines were reversed for the inaugural event. The first 18-hole play-off took place in 1942.

The course was designed by Jones and English-born Alister MacKenzie (1870–1934).

ANOTHER FIRST AT THE US MASTERS WAS: The FIRST hole-in-one was hit by Ross Somerville on the 16th hole with a mashie at the first tournament.

—•—•◦•—•—

THE FIRST
PLAYER TO WIN
ALL FOUR MAJOR
WORLD CHAMPIONSHIPS

GENE SARAZEN AT US MASTERS, AUGUSTA NATIONAL GOLF CLUB, 2604 WASHINGTON ROAD, AUGUSTA, GEORGIA, USA. MONDAY 8 APRIL 1935

Born on 27 February 1902 at Harrison, New York as Eugenio Saraceni, he became Gene Sarazen because, he said, he did not want to be mistaken for a violinist. It was only when he contracted pleurisy that Sarazen took up golf – he had to stop working as an apprentice carpenter to his father when he was advised to find a less strenuous job and began playing golf to relax. His career began when he was 17 and he changed his name.

He won the US Open on 15 July 1922 the same year that he also took the US PGA title (18 August 1922, on the West Course at Oakmont Country Club, Pennsylvania) and held on to it the following year (29 September 1923 at Pelham) when he was also expected to triumph at Troon in his first attempt at The Open but failed even to qualify.

In 1924 he came joint 41st and did not enter after that for a number of years but came second in 1928. He finally won the competition when it was held at Prince's Golf Club, Sandwich, Kent for the first time in 1932, by a margin of five shots. When he returned to defend his title, he came third, 21st in 1934, didn't play in 1935, was fifth in 1936, his last attempt.

Back home he won the US Open on 25 June 1932 at Fresh Meadow Country Club, New York by three strokes from Bobby Cruickshank. In

April 1935 he won the US Masters to complete victory in all four Major world championships. Sarazen went round in 282 strokes (68–71–73–70), the same as Craig Wood, but Sarazen won the play-off by 144 to 149.

Ten years earlier, he had won the Metropolitan Open and the year after the Miami Open which he retained in 1927, 1928 and 1929, the year he won the Miami Beach Open for the second successive time. In 1930 he had eight PGA Tour victories and narrowly lost the PGA Championship to Tommy Armour. On 13 August 1933 he won his third US PGA title beating Willie Goggin 5 and 4 at Blue Mound Country Club, Milwaukee, Wisconsin. Sarazen won 39 PGA Tour championships and played in six Ryder Cup teams (1927, 1929, 1931, 1933, 1935 and 1937). He died at Naples, Florida, aged 97 on 13 May 1999.

ALSO AT THIS MATCH: This was the LAST Major tournament win by Gene Sarazen

THE ONLY
PLAYER TO WIN THE
AMATEUR CHAMPIONSHIP AND US AMATEUR CHAMPIONSHIP
TWICE

W. LAWSON LITTLE, AMATEUR CHAMPIONSHIP AT 2 LINKS ROAD, PRESTWICK, STRATHCLYDE, SCOTLAND. 1934; US AMATEUR CHAMPIONSHIP AT THE COUNTRY CLUB, 191 CLYDE STREET, CHESTNUT HILL, MASSACHUSETTS, USA. SEPTEMBER 1934; AMATEUR CHAMPIONSHIP AT ROYAL LYTHAM & ST ANNES GOLF CLUB, LINKS GATE, LYTHAM ST ANNES, LANCASHIRE, ENGLAND. 1935; US AMATEUR CHAMPIONSHIP AT THE COUNTRY CLUB, 2825 LANDER ROAD, CLEVELAND, OHIO, USA. SEPTEMBER 1935

W. Lawson Little (1910–1968) set a record in 1935 when he became the only man to win both the Amateur Championship and US Amateur Championship twice. He won the British title at Royal Lytham beating Dr William Tweddell in the final by one hole. In the USA at the Country Club in Cleveland, Ohio he beat W. Emery by 4 and 2. The previous year he won the Amateur title beating J. Wallace by 13 and 14 and was victorious in the American Amateur beating D. Goldman 8 and 7.

THE LAST

PLAYER TO WIN A
MAJOR CHAMPIONSHIP WITH
HICKORY-SHAFTED
GOLF CLUBS

**Johnny Fischer, US Amateur Championship at Garden City Golf
Club, 206 Stewart Avenue, Garden City, New York, USA.
September 1936**

Johnny Fischer beat Jack McLean to win the US Amateur Championship,
but at one stage Fischer was 1 down with 3 to play. He saved the 34th with
a dead stymie and won the match on the 37th.

THE FIRST

WOMAN TO PLAY
IN A MEN'S
PROFESSIONAL
GOLF TOURNAMENT

BABE ZAHARIAS, LOS ANGELES OPEN, GRIFFITH PARK, LOS FELIZ, 4730
CRYSTAL SPRINGS DRIVE, LOS ANGELES, CALIFORNIA, USA. JANUARY 1938.

Mildred Ella 'Babe' Didriksen Zaharias was born at Port Arthur, Texas on
26 June 1911, the daughter of Norwegian immigrants. She changed the
spelling of her surname to Didrikson.

A veritable Renaissance woman, she won the sewing championship at
the 1931 State Fair of Texas in Dallas and later made many of the clothes
that she wore. The following year, she won two gold medals and one

silver medal for track and field in the 1932 Los Angeles Olympics (see page 118).

In 1933, she took up golf after being introduced to the game by the sports journalist Grantland Rice. She hit up to 1,000 balls each day to practise her swing, often leaving her hands covered in blisters. However, the game's authorities refused to let her take amateur status because she had allowed an interview and photograph to be used in an advertising campaign for a car, so in January 1938, she competed in the Los Angeles Open, a men's US PGA tournament. She shot 81 and 84 and missed the cut. At the tournament she met George Zaharias (1908–1984) and they were married two days before Christmas of that year. (Her marriage did nothing to quell rumours that she was a lesbian. Her closest friend was fellow golfer Betty Dodd.)

In the early 1940s the authorities agreed that she was indeed an amateur and she began competing in various tournaments. In 1945, Zaharias played in three PGA tournaments. She won the 1946 US Women's Amateur Golf Championship at Southern Hills beating Clara Sherman 11 and 9 in the 36-hole final and the Ladies' British Open Amateur Championship at Gullane on 12 June 1947, the first American to do so.

In 1947 she turned professional and dominated the Women's Professional Golf Association and later the Ladies Professional Golf Association, of which she was a founding member. She won the 1947 Titleholders Championship and the 1948 US Women's Open by eight strokes despite the bad weather. In 1946 and 1947 she won 17 straight women's amateur victories, a feat unequalled by anyone, male or female. In 1950 she completed the Grand Slam of the three women's Majors of the day, the US Open (by nine strokes), the Titleholders Championship, and the Western Open, as well as leading the money list. She was inducted into the Hall of Fame of Women's Golf in 1951.

She was not especially popular with her fellow competitors, since she knew she was much better than them. Despite her small stature she could hit a golf ball 250 yards (228 metres) with ease. When asked how she managed her amazing feat, she replied, 'You've got to loosen your girdle and let rip'. In 1953 she was diagnosed with colon cancer but won the US Women's Open championship in 1954 by an incredible 12 strokes over Betty Hicks, one month after surgery. It was her last appearance at the US

Women's Open championship because the cancer returned with a vengeance in 1955 and she died at the John Sealy Hospital in Galveston, Texas on 27 September 1956. She was just 45.

Including both her amateur and professional accomplishments, she won 82 golf tournaments. The Associated Press named her Athlete of the Year six times and the *Manchester Guardian* headlined its obituary of her 'Death of world's greatest athlete'. Of her, Grantland Rice wrote:

‘She is beyond all belief until you see her perform ... Then you finally understand that you are looking at the most flawless section of muscle harmony, of complete mental and physical coordination, the world of sport has ever seen.’

THE FIRST
TELEVISED
GOLF TOURNAMENT
ROEHAMPTON, ENGLAND. FRIDAY 15 JULY 1938

The BBC provided the first televised golf in 1938. On 17 January 1995 the Golf Channel was launched and the first live tournament on the channel was the Dubai Desert Classic, held from 19–22 January 1995.

THE LAST
OPEN TO DATE AT WHICH
BRITONS OCCUPIED THE
FIRST THREE PLACES
THE ROYAL ST GEORGE'S GOLF CLUB, SANDWICH, KENT, ENGLAND. WEDNESDAY 6–FRIDAY 8 JULY 1938

Reg Whitcombe took first place while Jimmy Adams was runner-up and Henry Cotton came in third. Whitcombe went round in 295 (71–71–75–78) while Adams rook 297 strokes (70–71–78–78) and Cotton one more 298 (74–73–77–74). In 1939 Dick Burton became the last Briton, to date, to win the Claret Jug at The Open at St Andrews. He went round the course in 290 strokes (70–72–77–71).

THE ONLY

PLAYER TO LOSE
THE US OPEN FOR
TEEING OFF
TOO EARLY

ED 'PORKY' OLIVER, CANTERBURY GOLF CLUB, 22000 SOUTH WOODLAND ROAD, CLEVELAND, OHIO, USA. SUNDAY 9 JUNE 1940

In 1940 Gene Sarazen was determined to win the US Open, 18 years after his first victory. As it turned out, he lost a play-off to Lawson Little. If things had been different, the play-off may have been a three-way fight as Ed 'Porky' Oliver (1916–1961) also recorded the same final score as Sarazen and Little – 287. Known as Porky because he weighed 238 lb (108 kg) yet stood only 5 ft 9 in (1.7 metres), Oliver and five other golfers – Johnny Bulla, Duke Gibson, Claude Harmon, Ky Laffoon and Dutch Harrison – began their final round 28 minutes ahead of their scheduled tee time because they wanted to avoid getting caught in a thunderstorm. The organizing committee did not think this a proper excuse and disqualified all six players. Porky Oliver died of cancer on 21 September 1961, 15 days after his 45th birthday.

THE ONLY
LADIES' BRITISH OPEN AMATEUR CHAMPION
TO SERVE IN THE
BATTLE OF BRITAIN

PAM BARTON, KENT, ENGLAND. SEPTEMBER 1940

Born on 4 March 1917 at 118 Castelnau, Barnes, Surrey, Pamela Espeut Barton began playing golf when she was 12 and won the French

International Ladies Golf Championship aged 17. That year (1934), she was also the runner-up in the Ladies' British Open Amateur Championship, won the French championship at Le Touquet and was chosen to play for Great Britain against France at Chantilly.

The following year Barton was also runner-up and made her debut for England – she played in all of the international matches from 1935 to 1939.

Finally in 1936, she won the Ladies' British Open Amateur Championship beating Bridget Newell in the final at Southport and Ainsdale, and a few months later in the autumn she won the US Women's Amateur Golf Championship at the Canoe Brook Country Club in Summit, New Jersey beating Maureen Orcutt 4 and 3 in the 36-hole final, to become only the second lady to have won both British and American ladies' championships in the same year. (Dorothy Campbell had achieved the double in 1909. It would be another 30 years after Barton before Catherine Lacoste repeated the feat.) Barton was just 19. In 1934 and 1936 she competed for Great Britain in the Curtis Cup. In 1938 she was runner-up in the French Championship.

In 1939 Barton won her second Ladies' British Open Amateur Championship but on the declaration of war she joined up and served as an ambulance driver during the Battle of Britain. In the summer of 1941 she joined the Women's Auxiliary Air Force as a radio operator. She was soon commissioned and sent to RAF Manston in Kent.

On 13 November 1943 Barton was killed aged 26 in an aeroplane crash at RAF Detling. She had attended a dance with a pilot friend and the accident occurred early the next morning as they were preparing to fly home. She was buried in St John's Cemetery, Margate. Laddie Lucas wrote of her:

'Relatively short of stature and well built, Pam possessed, beneath a head of reddish hair, an engaging freckled face which mostly wore a smile. A warm friendliness, and a modesty which brushed success easily aside, drew people to her. A totally unaffected personality allowed her to devote her days to golf without people saying she had surrendered herself unreasonably to the game. It camouflaged an intense ambition to get to the top. And stay there.'

THE ONLY
MAN TO WIN THE
US OPEN
WEARING A CORSET

Craig Wood, US Open at Colonial Club, 3735 Country Club Circle,
Fort Worth, Texas, USA. Saturday 7 June 1941

Craig Wood (1901–1968), who had finished second in the US Open on
12 June 1939 and fourth on 9 June 1940, won the last tournament before
the Second World War stopped play (until 1946) by three strokes. He went
round in 284 (73–71–70–70) beating Densmore Shute into second place.
Wood had contemplated not entering the competition because he had a
bad back but decided to play on, albeit wearing a corset.

THE LAST
PGA TOUR
WIN BY
GENE SARAZEN

MIAMI BILTMORE INTERNATIONAL FOUR-BALL AT MIAMI BILTMORE GOLF
COURSE, 1200 ANASTASIA AVENUE, CORAL GABLES, FLORIDA, USA. 1941

Gene Sarazen won his 39th and last PGA Tour event (with Ben Hogan)
in 1941. The Miami International Four-Ball was part of the PGA Tour
from 1924 to 1954. Sarazen and Hogan were victorious over 15 other two-
man teams.

THE ONLY
OSCAR WINNER
TO DESTROY HIS
ACADEMY AWARD
WITH A GOLF CLUB

BARRY FITZGERALD. 1945

On 15 March 1945 Barry Fitzgerald won a Best Supporting Actor Oscar for his role as Father Fitzgibbon in *Going My Way* (released 2 October 1944). Fitzgerald was nominated by the Academy for both Best Actor and Best Supporting Actor awards for the same performance, the only time this has happened. During the Second World, owing to the rationing of metal, Oscars were made from plaster. One day Fitzgerald was at home practising his golf swing when he accidentally knocked the head off his precious trophy. Fortunately, for him the Academy of Motion Pictures, Arts & Sciences agreed to replace the Oscar.

THE FIRST
MAJOR WIN BY
SAM SNEAD

US PGA AT SEAVIEW COUNTRY CLUB, 401 SOUTH NEW
YORK ROAD, ABSECON, NEW JERSEY, USA.
SUNDAY 31 MAY 1942

On the day before both were due to report for military duty, sailor Sam Snead beat Corporal Jim Turnesa in the final of the 25th US PGA Championship by 2 and 1. At lunch, Snead, the favourite, was three holes down on the first 18 but after lunch he fought back to equal the scores on the 27th hole. Snead won the match and the tournament on the 35th with a birdie, to win his first Major competition.

THE ONLY
WINNER OF A PROFESSIONAL GOLF TOURNAMENT AND WIMBLEDON MEN'S TENNIS CHAMPIONSHIP

Ellsworth Vines. Southern California Open Championship, California, USA. 1945; Men's Singles Championship, Church Road, Wimbledon, London, England. Saturday 2 July 1932

Born at Los Angeles, California on 28 September 1911, Henry Ellsworth Vines Jr. was a talented tennis player, winning Wimbledon Men's Singles Championship in 1932 beating Bunny Austin 6–4, 6–2, 6–0 and the US Open Men's Singles Championship on 12 September 1931 and 3 September 1932 at Forest Hills. He reached the Wimbledon final in 1933 and played his first professional tennis match on 10 January 1934. He won his last tournament, the US Pro Championship at Beverly Hills Tennis Club on 22 October 1939 and played his last match in May 1940 when 28 years old, before turning his hand to golf having become bored with tennis. He became a professional golfer in 1942 and three years later won the Southern California Open Championship. He died on St Patrick's Day, 1994.

THE FIRST
US WOMEN'S OPEN

Spokane Country Club, 2010 West Waikiki Road, Spokane, Washington, USA. Sunday 1 September 1946

The US Women's Open began in 1946 but was not adopted by the United States Golf Association until 1953 when 17 of the 37 entrants were professionals. The first winner was Patty Berg. Born at Minneapolis, Minnesota Patty Berg (1918–2006) began playing golf in 1931 and, three years later, entered amateur competitions winning the Minneapolis City Championship. In 1935 she was runner-up to Glenna Collett-Vare in the US Women's Amateur Championship. She won the Titleholders Championship in 1937 and the US Women's Amateur Championship in 1938 at Westmoreland. Berg became a professional in 1940 but served as a lieutenant in the US Marines for three years from 1942. On demob, she won the inaugural US Women's Open in 1946 beating Betty Jameson 5 and 4 in the final. In 1957 the competitors were told to wear skirts rather than shorts, apparently to conform to a club rule at Winged Foot, New York.

THE FIRST
AMERICAN WOMAN
TO WIN THE
LADIES' BRITISH OPEN
AMATEUR CHAMPIONSHIP

BABE DIDRIKSON, LADIES' BRITISH OPEN AMATEUR CHAMPIONSHIP AT DUNCUR ROAD, MUIRFIELD, GULLANE, EAST LOTHIAN, SCOTLAND.
THURSDAY 12 JUNE 1947

Mildred Ella 'Babe' Didrikson Zaharias was forced to become a professional in 1935 because she had been a professional athlete in the 1930s and so became the first woman to compete in a man's competition. In 1947 she became the first American to win the Ladies' British Open Amateur Championship. Immediately after, she became a professional once again.

THE FIRST
BLACK PLAYERS
IN A PROFESSIONAL
GOLF TOURNAMENT

TED RHODES AND BILL SPILLER, RIVIERA COUNTRY CLUB, LOS ANGELES OPEN, 1250 CAPRI DRIVE, PACIFIC PALISADES, CALIFORNIA, USA. 1948

Ted Rhodes (1913–1969) and Bill Spiller (1913–1988) became the first black players to compete in a professional tournament when they participated in the 1948 Los Angeles Open. At the time the policy of the Professional Golfers' Association of America (PGA) was to leave the decision whether to allow non-whites up to the individual tournament's sponsors. Spiller finished 33rd and Rhodes two places behind him.

Rhodes and Spiller then sued the PGA to force the association to drop the 1943 clause in its constitution that allowed only white players to participate in competitions. They claimed that by preventing black players from competing they were guilty of restraint of trade. The PGA settled out of court not long before the case was due to be heard, by promising to end discrimination. However, the association managed to avoid agreeing to the settlement by making all its competitions invitation-only and only inviting white players to compete.

It was not until November 1961 that the PGA dropped the colour bar after California attorney general (and future California Supreme Court justice) Stanley Mosk threatened to ban the PGA from using all public and private courses. In 2009 the PGA awarded posthumous memberships to Rhodes and Spiller.

DEMOB MATES

On demob after the Second World War, Ted Rhodes met and befriended Billy Eckstine, the showbusiness entertainer, and Joe Louis, the heavyweight boxing champion. He taught both men how to play golf and later became the personal coach, valet and playing partner of Louis.

THE FIRST

PGA
PLAYER OF THE YEAR

BEN HOGAN, 1948

Ben Hogan was named the first PGA Player of the Year. From 1990 there have also been awards for PGA Tour Player of the Year, PGA Tour Rookie of the Year and from 1991 Comeback Player of the Year.

THE FIRST

RECIPIENT OF
US MASTERS
GREEN JACKET

SAM SNEAD, US MASTERS AT AUGUSTA NATIONAL GOLF CLUB, 2604 WASHINGTON ROAD, AUGUSTA, GEORGIA, USA. SUNDAY 10 APRIL 1949.

The first green jacket was awarded to Sam Snead, winner of the US Masters in 1949. As well as money, the winner of the US Masters is presented with a green jacket that he can keep for a year before returning it to the Augusta National Golf Club. The coat is the official one worn by members of the golf club when they are on club premises and every Masters winner automatically becomes an honorary club member. After the year is up the champion is supposed to return the jacket to Augusta where it is kept for him to wear the following year during the next Masters.

In 1962, the year after he won the US Masters, South African Gary Player did not return his green jacket despite being asked repeatedly by

A LONG WAIT

It took Jack Nicklaus 35 years to get his own green jacket after winning the US Masters. He won the title on 7 April 1963 and as detailed above the club picked out a jacket for him to wear at the presentation ceremony until one could be made. The jacket chosen for him in 1963 was a 46 long but since Nicklaus wore a 44 regular, it was too big for him. The tailor at Augusta measured Nicklaus for his own jacket but when he returned the club was embarrassed to reveal that they had forgotten to have the jacket made so Nicklaus wore the only one on the premises that fitted him – one that had belonged to New York governor Thomas E. Dewey. Nicklaus wore the jacket until 1972 when he had his own tailor, Hart, Schaffner and Marx, run one up. The only problems were that the garment was the wrong material and the wrong colour. In 1997 Nicklaus mentioned the problem to Augusta's then-chairman Jack Stephens who insisted that the matter be rectified immediately. However, it as another year before Nicklaus finally got around to being measured – 35 years after his first victory.

the Augusta officials. 'I wasn't aware of the rules and regulations and I naturally assumed the green jacket was like a trophy, so I brought it home with me to South Africa,' explained Player. '[Masters co-founder] Clifford Roberts called me and told me in no uncertain terms that the green jacket was not to leave club grounds. I invited him to South Africa for a visit and he could bring it back. I don't think he was amused. He told me just to make sure I brought it back the following spring.' Although Player returned the following year to Augusta, the jacket stayed in South Africa.

The jacket is made from 55 per cent wool and 45 per cent polyester and its official colour is Masters Green. The crest of the Augusta National Golf Club is on the left breast pocket and also on the brass buttons. As each US Masters nears its end, club officials pick a number of jackets that they think might fit the eventual winner at the presentation ceremony. After the winner is known, a tailor takes his measurements and a bespoke jacket is prepared. If a player wins a second US Masters, he does not receive another green jacket unless his body shape has altered dramatically.

THE ONLY
MAJOR DECIDED BY
BROKEN GLASS

THE OPEN AT THE ROYAL ST GEORGE'S GOLF CLUB, SANDWICH, KENT, ENGLAND. FRIDAY 8 JULY 1949

At The Open in 1949 Bobby Locke beat genial Irishman Harry Bradshaw in play-off by 12 strokes to win the Claret Jug. Things may have been different had Bradshaw not driven his ball into a pile of broken glass on the fifth hole in the second round. The Rules of Golf have since been changed but at the time Bradshaw had no option but to play the ball and the glass. Also, Bradshaw was a man of principle who did not want to hold up proceedings or take a possibly unfair, as he saw it, advantage. He closed his eyes and played a stroke with his wedge. For his troubles, he received a shower of glass in the face including a piece that lodged in his eye. To add insult to injury, he managed only to hit the ball 20 yards (18 metres) and scored a double bogey on the hole. The incident troubled him and he finished the round on 77. The next day he shot 68 and 70 to go with his first round 68 and 77 but it was only enough to tie him with Bobby Locke. Reports have long stated that the ball landed in the bottom half of a broken beer bottle but these arose because an enterprising photographer put a ball in a broken beer bottle and claimed that was the way the ball lay.

THE ONLY
PLAYER TO LOSE THE US OPEN
BECAUSE OF A GNAT

LLOYD MANGRUM, US OPEN AT MERION CRICKET CLUB, 325 MONTGOMERY AVENUE, HAVERFORD, PENNSYLVANIA, USA. SUNDAY 11 JUNE 1950

At the end of the normal play, Lloyd Mangrum, Ben Hogan and George Fazio were all tied on 287 strokes at Merion Cricket Club. A play-off followed and Hogan scored 69 to Mangrum's 73 and Fazio's 75 to take the title. It could have been so different if a gnat had not landed on Mangrum's ball as he was about to take a putt. Without thinking of the possible consequences, he picked up the ball to get rid of the gnat. Mangrum was penalized two strokes, two strokes without which he would have won the US Open.

THE LAST
MAJOR TOURNAMENT WON BY BYRON NELSON

BING CROSBY PRO-AM AT PEBBLE BEACH, CALIFORNIA, USA.
FRIDAY 12–SUNDAY 14 JANUARY 1951.

Born near Waxahachie, Texas in 1912 John Byron Nelson Jr. barely survived typhoid fever as a small boy and lost half his body weight. Aged 12, he began caddying at the Glen Garden Country Club where it was strictly forbidden for caddies to play so Nelson would sneak back after dark to practise, placing white handkerchiefs over the holes. When the club changed its policy, Nelson played a match in the Glen Garden Caddie Tournament against fellow future champ Ben Hogan and won by one stroke over nine holes.

Nelson joined the US PGA tour in 1935 and won the New Jersey State Open. He won tournaments every year (apart from 1943) until 1946. His most successful year was 1945 when he won 18 competitions including 11 consecutively: San Francisco Victory Open, Knoxville War Bond Tournament, New York Red Cross Tourney, Minneapolis Four-Ball (with Harold 'Jug' McSpaden), Tam O'Shanter Open, Nashville Open, Texas Victory Open and the San Francisco Open. In 1945 Nelson's stroke average was 68.33. He won the US Masters on 4 April 1937 and 13 April 1942. He won the US Open on 12 June 1939 and the US PGA Championship on 2 September 1940 and 15 July 1945.

The last tournament he entered and won was the 1951 Bing Crosby Pro-Am with a score of 209 (71–67–71) to beat golfing dentist Dr Cary Middlecoff by three shots, 212 (76–67–69). Ed Furgol, George Fazio and Julius Boros tied for third at 213. Nelson took home $2,000 in prize money. The players practised on Thursday and it rained but it stayed dry for the three days of the tournament. The competition was 54 holes over three different courses and there was no cut.

THE ONLY
OCCASION THE OPEN
WAS NOT HELD ON THE
BRITISH
MAINLAND

THE OPEN AT ROYAL PORTRUSH, DUNLUCE ROAD, PORTRUSH, COUNTY ANTRIM, NORTHERN IRELAND. FRIDAY 6 JULY 1951

On just one occasion has The Open been staged outside of mainland Great Britain and that was in the summer of 1951 when it was played at Royal Portrush in County Antrim. Jimmy Adams was the first-round leader after a stunning 68 but slipped into fifth place by the time he had shot his four rounds. Max Faulkner, who was reputed to have bet on himself to win, moved into a two-shot lead on 141 at the end of the second round ahead of Norman Sutton. On the last morning, Faulkner hit 70 and then a 74 to finish on 285.

The last player on the green was Argentinian Antonio Cerdá who went out in 34. Cerdá needed to finish the last three holes in 12 to tie with Faulkner but was unable to achieve that and took 14 strokes, giving the Claret Jug to the Englishman.

THE ONLY

GOLFERS KILLED BY US NAVY

JACKSONVILLE, FLORIDA, USA. TUESDAY 18 MARCH 1952

Thankfully, it is not often that golfers are killed by the military – even accidentally. Two lady golfers were playing on a course at Jacksonville, Florida in the spring of 1952 when a crippled navy fighter with a dead engine coming in to land hit them with its propeller, killing them instantly.

THE FIRST

WORLD CUP

The Canada Cup at Beaconsfield Golf Club, 49 avenue Golf, Pointe-Claire, Québec, Canada. Tuesday 2–Wednesday 3 June 1953

The Canada Cup – the game's oldest worldwide team competition – was founded in 1953 by the American industrialist John Jay Hopkins 'for the furtherance of good fellowship and better understanding among the nations of the world through the medium of international golf competition'. Each country would be represented by two players playing 72 holes of stroke play, their combined scores producing a team total.

In 2000, the year that it became part of the World Golf Championship and organized by the International Golf Federation of PGA Tours, the format was changed to alternate between four balls and foursomes. Among the participants over the years have been Severiano Ballesteros, Ernie Els, Nick Faldo, Bernhard Langer, Johnny Miller, Jack Nicklaus, Arnold Palmer, Gary Player, Sam Snead, Peter Thomson and Tiger Woods (who won it for America in 2000).

The first Canada Cup was won by the Argentine team consisting of Roberto De Vicenzo and Antonio Cerdá. With a score of 287, they beat eight other countries. Canada finished second with 297 strokes. In 1966 the name of the trophy was changed to the World Cup. Ironically, in November 1968 at the Olgiata Golf Club in Rome, Italy, Canada won the World Cup – a feat it never managed when the trophy was actually called the Canada Cup. Its two-man team of Al Balding and George Knudson beat the American team of Lee Trevino and Julius Boros by two shots – 569 to 571.

THE LAST
MAJOR TOURNAMENT WIN BY BEN HOGAN

THE OPEN AT CARNOUSTIE GOLF CLUB, 3 LINKS PARADE, CARNOUSTIE, ANGUS, SCOTLAND. FRIDAY 10 JULY 1953

On the foggy Texas morning of 2 February 1949 Ben Hogan, then 46, was involved in a car crash that left him hospitalized for a month. His vehicle smacked headlong into a Greyhound bus outside Van Horn in the Lone Star state and Hogan threw himself across his wife to protect her. He saved both their lives but in the process he suffered a double fracture of the pelvis, a fractured collarbone, a chipped rib, a fractured left ankle and several blood clots that had him hovering near death. His surgeons told Hogan that he would probably never walk again let alone play golf.

They reckoned without his determination, and the following year he battled to play in the Ryder Cup in England and that year he also won the US Masters and the US Open and retained the title the following year. In 1952 he came third but 1953 proved to be his best year. On 12 April he won the US Masters with a total of 274 (70–69–66–69), which was the lowest score until 1965.

His next triumph came at the US Open at Oakmont on 13 June which he led from the start, the first player to do so for 42 years. He finished with a par and two birdies to win by six strokes over Sam Snead – the biggest margin since 1938.

Initially reluctant to travel to Britain for The Open, Hogan was eventually persuaded to make the journey. As was his wont, he prepared thoroughly and arrived a fortnight before the tournament was due to start. He practised with the smaller ball then in use in Britain and returned figures of 73–71–70–68 to win the Claret Jug. It was the only time he entered The Open. He was unable to participate in the US PGA Championship and thus possibly achieve the Grand Slam because The Open and the US PGA overlapped. Hogan perhaps should have retired after his triple triumphs but the passion for golf burned deep within him and he continued until 1967. He died on 25 July 1997.

THE FIRST
US GOLF TOURNAMENT
SHOWN ON
NATIONAL TELEVISION

The Tam O'Shanter World Championship Of Golf at Tam O'Shanter Country Club, 6700 West Howard Street, Niles, Illinois, USA. August 1953

The first televised Tam O'Shanter World Championship came to network television because George S. May paid ABC $32,000 to broadcast a one-hour special. Around a million people watched the view from a single camera located above the grandstand on the 18th green. With ten minutes of the programme left Lew Worsham, trailing by one shot, holed a 104-yard (95-metre) wedge shot (some sources say 115 yards/105 metres) from the fairway on the final hole for eagle and victory and $25,000.

George S. May, born on a farm in Windsor, Illinois in 1890, bought the Tam O'Shanter Country Club in 1936 after a fire destroyed the clubhouse. In the following years, May invested more than $500,000 to renovate and operate the facility. In 1941 he began to sponsor golf tournaments mainly due to unhappiness with his experience at the US Open held at Canterbury Country Club in Cleveland on 9 June 1940.

The first Tam O'Shanter Open, held in 1941, offered $15,000, then the largest purse in professional golf. George May reduced admission prices to $1 from the $3.30 charged by the Canterbury Country Club. May was also innovative in providing grandstands at key locations around the course as well as shortwave radio broadcasts so that fans could follow events happening elsewhere. He also sold hot dogs, burgers, beers and soft drinks.

After the tournament was finished, he hosted a dance and made slot machines available. More than 41,000 spectators attended the event including 23,000 on the last day. *The Saturday Evening Post*'s reporter wrote, 'All told, it was a cross between a county fair and a good airplane crash.'

In 1945, May launched the Tam O'Shanter World Championship of Golf, offering a total purse of $60,000 in war bonds, with the winner receiving $13,600. He was the first to allow club members to use golf carts and to install telephones at each tee for members to use. One failure was the refusal of golfers to wear numbers so that fans could track them. He paid one golfer to wear a mask so he could be billed as the Masked Marvel and he gave money to Scottish golfers to play in kilts. The tournament proved popular with the public and less than popular with the golf establishment. George May died of a heart at the Tam O'Shanter Country Club at the age of 71 on 12 March 1962.

THE FIRST
WINNER OF THE
VARE TROPHY
PATTY BERG. 1953.

The Vare Trophy is presented to the professional lady golfer who has scored the lowest average number of strokes, which is ironic because the lady after whom the trophy is named won most of her tournaments in matchplay.

To be eligible the player must have participated in a minimum of 70 LPGA tournament rounds. The trophy is named for Glenna Collett-Vare who was known as the female Bobby Jones and the 'Queen of American Golf'.

Born at New Haven, Connecticut in 1903, Collett Vare was raised in Providence, Rhode Island. Considering today's precocity among golfers, she did not start playing the game till she was 14 but soon progressed and won the US Women's Amateur Championship when she was 19. USGA president Richard Tufts said of her, 'Glenna was the first woman to attack the hole rather than just to play to the green.' In 1923 she won the Canadian Women's Amateur Golf Championship. In 1924 she won 59 out of 60 matches, losing once and that by fluke when in the semi-final of the US Women's Amateur Mary K. Browne's ball bounced off Vare's and into the hole. Rival player Enid Wilson said, 'Her vigorous game set up an entirely fresh standard for her countrywomen, and the young up-and-coming golfers in the 1930s were inspired by her example.'

Collett Vare won the US Women's Amateur Championship again in 1925, and then again in 1928, 1929 and 1930. In 1929 and 1930 she came second in the Ladies' British Open Amateur Golf Championship. Her sixth and last US Women's Amateur Championship came in 1935 when she was a 32-year-old mother of two and she beat 17-year-old Patty Berg. Collett Vare played for America in the first Curtis Cup played at the Wentworth Golf Club in England in 1932 and was player-captain in 1934, 1936, 1938, and 1948. Her last title was the 1959 Rhode Island Women's Golf Association championship. Of her own game, Collett Vare once said:

'To make oneself a successful match-player, there are certain qualities to be sought after, certain ideas must be kept in mind, and certain phases of one's attitude towards the game that come in for special notice. The three I have taken are these: love of combat, serenity of mind and fearlessness.'

The woman called by Gene Sarazen 'the greatest woman golfer of all time' died aged 85 on 3 February 1989 at Gulfstream, Florida.

The first winner of the Vare Trophy was Patty Berg (1918–2006) who was beaten by Collett Vare to win her last amateur title.

THE ONLY
GOLF COURSE WITH
LANDMINES
IN THE ROUGH

CAMP BONIFAS, KOREA. 1953.

Created in 1953, Camp Bonifas is located in the demilitarized border between South and North Korea. Originally named Camp Kitty Hawk and Camp Liberty Bell, it was rededicated on 18 August 1986 after Captain Arthur G. Bonifas, who was murdered by North Korean troops on 18 August 1976. The camp has a one-hole par 3 golf course called by *Sports Illustrated* 'the most dangerous hole in golf' because it is surrounded by land mines. A sign on the course bears the legend, 'Danger! Do not retrieve balls from the rough. Live mine fields.' Civilians are not allowed to play and military personnel are known to take a drop.

THE FIRST
BEST-SELLING
GOLF BOOK

HOW TO PLAY YOUR BEST GOLF ALL THE TIME BY TOMMY ARMOUR, USA. 1953.

The book was written by Tommy Armour, who had won The US Open in a play-off on 17 June 1927 when it was held at the Oakmont Country Club in Pennsylvania. Armour beat Harry Cooper in a play-off by 76 to 79, holing a 10 ft (3 metre) birdie putt on the 72nd green. On 13

IRON FINGERS

Tommy Armour had tremendous strength in his arms. Using only his thumb and forefinger, he was able to hold a billiard cue by its tip at arm's length.

September 1930 Armour won the US Professional Golfers' Association Championship, triumphing over Gene Sarazen by one hole in the final. The following year he won the Claret Jug, the first time The Open was held at Carnoustie.

His career went downhill afterwards, and on his retirement Armour became a teacher at Congressional Club in Washington, then opened a golf school at Winged Foot, New York in the summer and Boca Raton, Florida in the winter. He would arrive at the course by 8 am and take a seat next to a table with a generous supply of gin and tonic. From this vantage point, he would coach his pupils until 12.30 pm when he moved to the bar to entertain members and guests with his golfing anecdotes. Then, after a good lunch, he would challenge holidaying golfers to matches for $50 or $100 each half, and the same for the round. It was only on very rare occasions that he lost. Armour later used the techniques as the basis for his book which became the first best-seller on the game and is still in print today. The journalist Ross Goodner said of the man:

'Nothing was ever small about Tommy Armour's reputation. At one time or another, he was known as the greatest iron player, the greatest raconteur, the greatest drinker and the greatest and most expensive teacher in golf.'

A follow-up volume, *A Round of Golf with Tommy Armour*, was published six years later. It was also said that Armour liked to shoot chipmunks with a .22 calibre rifle during his lessons. The worse a player, the more chipmunks were shot. One of his pupils was unhappy with this state of affairs but only because he felt Armour was not paying enough attention. 'When are you going to stop doing that and take care of me?' he asked plaintively. Armour replied, 'Don't tempt me.' According to the Ian Fleming novel *Diamonds are Forever*, one of James Bond's favourite books is *How to Play Your Best Golf all the Time*. Armour died at Larchmont, New York, on 11 September 1968 (see 1927, page 109).

THE FIRST

GOLF TOURNAMENT
TO OFFER A
SIX-FIGURE PURSE

THE TAM O'SHANTER WORLD CHAMPIONSHIP OF GOLF AT TAM O'SHANTER COUNTRY CLUB, 6700 WEST HOWARD STREET, NILES, ILLINOIS, USA. AUGUST 1954

The Tam O'Shanter World Championship of Golf in its latter years offered more prize money than any other tournament including The US Open. The competition was devised by George S. May. Beginning in 1946, the Tam O'Shanter was a 36-hole, winner-take-all exhibition event with prizes of $10,000. In 1949 it became a 72-hole tournament and in 1952 the prize money began to increase. The winner took home $25,000 in 1952 and 1953, and starting in 1954, $50,000 with an additional $50,000 available in the form of a contract with George S. May for 50 worldwide exhibition events. The first $50,000 prize winner was Bob Toski. To give some idea of the difference between the Tam O'Shanter and other competitions, in his three other tournament victories on the PGA Tour in 1954 Toski won $8,000. For all competitions that year Toski won $65,819.81 and the man in second place, Jack Burke Jr., earned just $20,000.

THE FIRST

AUSTRALIAN
TO WIN THE OPEN

Peter Thomson, The Open at Royal Birkdale Golf Club, Waterloo Road, Southport, Merseyside, England. Friday 9 July 1954

Born at Melbourne, Australia on 23 August 1929, Peter Thomson was training as an industrial chemist when he gave it up to become a professional golfer. He won his first Open in 1954 with a score of 283 (72–71–69–71) and then dominated the tournament for five years: winning on 8 July 1955 on the Old Course at St Andrews going round in 281 (71–68–70–72); 6 July 1956 at Hoylake hitting 286 (70–70–72–74); and 4 July 1958 at Royal Lytham with a score of 278 (66–72–67–73). He is the only player in modern times to win the Claret Jug three years in a row. He also won The Open on 9 July 1965, again at Royal Birkdale. He went round in 285 (74–68–72–71).

The Birkdale Golf Club opened in 1889 and received the Royal seal of approval in 1951. It should have held The Open for the first time in 1940 but was prevented from doing so by the Second World War. The first time the club hosted an important tournament was the Amateur Championship in May 1946. The rainy, windswept final was between James Bruen and Robert Sweeny. Bruen won thanks in no small measure to his putting ability by 4 and 3. The competition was also judged a success because in the clubhouse bars were large quantities of Scotch – then in short supply – which could be bought by visitors as well as members.

ALSO A FIRST AT THIS MATCH: The FIRST Open held at Royal Birkdale

THE FIRST
BRIDGE AT
US MASTERS
DEDICATED TO A PLAYER

SARAZEN BRIDGE, THE US MASTERS AT AUGUSTA NATIONAL GOLF CLUB, 2604 WASHINGTON ROAD, AUGUSTA, GEORGIA, USA. WEDNESDAY 6 APRIL 1955

There are three bridges at the US Masters course at Atlanta dedicated to players. The first is dedicated to Gene Sarazen and is near the 15th green where Sarazen's 'shot heard round the world' took place, when using a 4-wood he hit a double eagle at the 485-yard par five 15th that helped him tie with Craig Wood after 72 holes of the Masters on the cold, wet afternoon of 7 April 1935. The next day, Sarazen won the title on a 36-hole play-off. 'I took my stance with my 4-wood and rode into the shot with every ounce of strength and timing I could muster. The split second I hit the ball I knew it would carry the pond. It tore for the flag on a very low trajectory, no more than 30 feet in the air,' he recalled. Sarazen did not see the ball go into the cup but heard the crowd reaction, which was enough to tell him that he had done it. 'Usually, they applaud when you hit a good shot. When they start jumping and running for the green, it is different.' The other two bridges were dedicated to Byron Nelson and Ben Hogan on 2 April 1958.

THE FIRST

NON-AMERICAN PLAYER
TO WIN THE
US WOMEN'S OPEN

FAY CROCKER, US WOMEN'S OPEN AT WICHITA COUNTRY CLUB, 8501 EAST 13TH STREET NORTH, WICHITA, KANSAS, USA. SUNDAY 3 JULY 1955

The first non-American woman to win the US Women's Open was not a Briton, a continental European or even an Antipodean but a Uruguayan. Fay Crocker came from Montevideo, Uruguay, where she was born in 1914, the daughter of an American expat who won the Uruguayan men's golf championship 27 times. A year after she turned professional, Crocker won the 1955 US Women's Open by four strokes (74-72-79-74 for 299) despite heavy winds of up to 40 mph. Favourite 'Babe' Didriksen Zaharias was unable to compete because of her cancer operation. The tournament was Crocker's first Major title.

Five years later, she won the Titleholders Championship, where she set a record as the oldest LPGA Major champion when she was well past her 45th birthday. She also won the Uruguayan women's national championship 20 times and the Argentinean national women's title 14 times.

THE FIRST

£1,000 FIRST PRIZE AT THE OPEN

THE OPEN AT ST ANDREWS, FIFE, SCOTLAND.
THURSDAY 7 JULY 1955

In what would be the second year of Peter Thomson's domination, the prize money for coming first hit the £1,000 mark for the first time and the BBC covered the tournament live for the first time.

ALSO AT THIS MATCH: The FIRST live coverage by the BBC of The Open

THE FIRST

WINNER OF THE BOB JONES AWARD

Francis Ouimet, USA. 1955

The Bob Jones Award is presented annually in recognition of 'a person who emulates Bob Jones's spirit, his personal qualities and his attitude toward the game and its players'. The first winner was Francis Ouimet (see 1913, page 91). The first female winner was Babe Zaharias in 1957, the year after her death from cancer. There have been some unexpected selections in the award winners. In 1978 the award was made jointly to Bing Crosby and Bob Hope, the first non-golfers to win, and in 2008 to President George W. Bush.

THE LAST

US PGA
MATCHPLAY CHAMPION

LIONEL HERBERT, US PGA CHAMPIONSHIP AT MIAMI VALLEY GOLF CLUB, 3311 SALEM AVENUE, DAYTON, OHIO, USA. SUNDAY 21 JULY 1957

From its inception in 1916 until 31 May 1942 and from 20 August 1944 until 21 July 1957 the US PGA Championship was a matchplay event. The 39th and last winner was Lionel Herbert who beat Dow Finsterwald by 3 and 1. Herbert went one up with a birdie at the 32nd and won with a par hole at the 35th. In 1958 at Llanerch Country Club in Pennsylvania the format was switched to a 72-hole medal play and was won by Dow Finsterwald. He went round in 276 (67–72–70–67) to win by two strokes.

THE LAST

TAM O'SHANTER
WORLD CHAMPIONSHIP
OF GOLF

THE TAM O'SHANTER WORLD CHAMPIONSHIP OF GOLF AT TAM O'SHANTER COUNTRY CLUB, CHICAGO, ILLINOIS, USA. AUGUST 1957

Beginning in 1946, the Tam O'Shanter World Championship of Golf offered more prize money than any other golf competition. It was devised by George S. May but in 1958 he decided to abandon the tournament after an argument with the US PGA over player entrance fees. The first winner had been Sam Snead and the last was Dick Mayer with Snead one of the runners-up.

THE LAST

MATCH PLAYED BY TELEPHONE

Cotswold Hills Golf Club, Cheltenham, Gloucestershire, England vs Cheltenham Golf Club, Melbourne, Victoria, Australia. 1957

In 1957 the last golf match conducted over the telephone was played. The match was open to all club members; and members of the Cotswold Hills Golf Club teed off in Cheltenham while their counterparts down under teed off in Melbourne. As the scores came in they were telephoned to the other club. The final result saw a victory for Cotswold Hills over Cheltenham by 564 to 570.

THE FIRST

GOLFER TO WIN BBC SPORTS PERSONALITY OF THE YEAR

DAI REES, GROSVENOR HOUSE HOTEL, 86 PARK LANE, LONDON, ENGLAND. DECEMBER 1957

First held on 30 December 1954 at the Savoy Hotel, the BBC Sports Personality of the Year was created by (Sir) Paul Fox and the first winner was athlete Christopher Chataway (the inaugural award was open only to athletes). The first golfer to win was David James 'Dai' Rees, CBE, who won in 1957, the year he captained the Great Britain Ryder Cup team to a 7.5–4.5 victory over the USA at Lindrick Golf Club in Yorkshire. It was America's sole defeat in the competition between 1933 and 1985. Rees captained the Great Britain Ryder Cup team five times: 1955 at Thunderbird Golf and Country Club, Palm Springs, California; 1957 at Lindrick Golf Club, Yorkshire; 1959 at Eldorado Country Club, Palm

---

WIN SOME, LOSE A LOT

As well as his triumphs Dai Rees is also the holder of an unwanted record. He appeared more times at The Open – 29 – without winning than any other player.

Desert, California; 1961 at Royal Lytham & St Annes, Lancashire; and 1967 at Champions Golf Club, Houston, Texas.

Rees won 39 competitions including four *News of the World Match Plays*, two British Masters, the Irish, Belgian and Swiss Opens, and the South African PGA Championship. Rees remained the only golfer to win the BBC title until Nick Faldo won it in 1989. Rees had died six years before on 10 September 1983, the result of a car crash some months earlier when he was on his way home from watching his favourite football team Arsenal.

THE FIRST

EISENHOWER TROPHY

St Andrews, Fife, Scotland. Wednesday 8-Monday 13 October 1958

The competition was a joint venture between the Royal & Ancient Golf Club and the US Golf Association organized in March 1958. The first tournament began seven months later with a trophy inscribed, 'To foster friendship and sportsmanship among the Peoples of the World'. Teams of four participate in stroke play with the best three scores of the four played counting and the lowest aggregate of the four leading to the winner. In the first competition Australia and the USA tied on 918 strokes each but the Aussies won the play-off 222 to 224. Great Britain and Ireland were one stroke behind to finish in joint third place. The Eisenhower Trophy is held every two years.

THE FIRST

GOLFER MADE FREEMAN OF ST ANDREWS

BOBBY JONES, ST ANDREWS, FIFE, SCOTLAND. 1958

In 1927 Bobby Jones won The Open at St Andrews by a clear six strokes (from Aubrey Boomer) and endeared himself to the public by asking for permission for the Claret Jug to remain at St Andrews rather than return with him to the USA.

Thirty-one years later, Jones became the first golfer to be made a Freeman of the city of St Andrews. He was also the second American so honoured; the first was Benjamin Franklin in 1759.

THE FIRST

PROFESSIONAL PLAYER TO BREAK 60

SAM SNEAD, GREENBRIER CLASSIC, WHITE SULPHUR SPRINGS, WEST VIRGINIA, USA. SATURDAY 16 MAY 1959

Slammin' Sam was the first professional to go around in fewer than 60 strokes when he went round in 59 at the unofficial Greenbrier Classic. He took 31 strokes on the front nine and 28 on the back nine. Snead took home a cheque for $4,500.

THE FIRST
BLACK PLAYER TO WIN A US NATIONAL CHAMPIONSHIP

Bill Wright, US Amateur Public Links, Welshire Golf Club, 3333 South Colorado Boulevard, Denver, Colorado, USA. July 1959

In the summer of 1959 Bill Wright won the US Amateur Public Links Tournament to become the first black player to win a national championship in America. In the final he beat Frank H. Campbell 3 and 2. Using two woods, nine irons and a putter, Wright saw off 2,434 other competitors.

THE ONLY
PROFESSIONAL FINED FOR FLATULENCE

TOMMY BOLT AT MEMPHIS INVITATIONAL OPEN, COLONIAL COUNTRY CLUB, 2736 COUNTRYWOOD PARKWAY, CORDOVA, TENNESSEE, USA. 1959

Known for his fierce temper, Tommy Bolt was waiting for his opponent to putt when he had a loud and sudden attack of flatulence. He was fined $250 for 'conduct unbecoming a professional golfer'.

THE FIRST
PLAYER TO WIN THE US WOMEN'S OPEN FOUR TIMES

BETSY RAWLS, US WOMEN'S OPEN AT WORCESTER COUNTRY CLUB, 2 RICE STREET, WORCESTER, MASSACHUSETTS, USA. 1960

In 1960 Betsy Rawls completed her fourth and final victory at the US Women's Open, having previously won in 1951, 1953 and 1957. Her third victory came under unusual circumstances because her score of 299 was not the lowest. That belonged to Jacqueline Pung who went round Winged Foot, New York in 298 but at one hole her marker put down the wrong score (six instead of a five) and she unknowingly endorsed the error by signing her card – a player is solely responsible for his or her score at any hole. Consequently, she was disqualified. The Winged Foot members, saddened by the error, held a collection for her and raised $3,000 – considerably more than the $1,800 actually won by Betsy Rawls. In 1960 Rawls went round in just 292 to win by one stroke.

ALSO AT WORCESTER COUNTRY CLUB: This club had also hosted the US Men's Open and so became the first venue to host both competitions.

THE FIRST

BLACK PLAYER TO GAIN FULL US PGA TOUR PLAYING PRIVILEGES

Charlie Sifford, US PGA Tour, USA. 1961

Born at Charlotte, North Carolina on 2 June 1922, Charlie Sifford began caddying when he was 13. He won the Negro National Open six times and in 1961 became the first full-time black player on the PGA Tour. In 1957 he won the Long Beach Open, which was not an official PGA Tour event, but was co-sponsored by the PGA. When he played in some tournaments, spectators would kick his ball into the rough, and he pulled out of the Greater Greensboro Open at Greensboro, North Carolina because of racist heckling.

In 1967, Sifford hit a 67 on the final round to win the Greater Hartford Open. Two years later, he won the Los Angeles Open. In 2004, Sifford became the first black player inducted into the World Golf Hall of Fame. Tiger Woods said, 'The pain, suffering and sacrifice experienced by Mr Sifford in being a lonely pioneer for black golfers on the PGA Tour will never be forgotten by me.'

THE FIRST
NON-AMERICAN
TO WIN US MASTERS
Gary Player, US Masters, Augusta National Golf Club, 2604
Washington Road, Augusta, Georgia, USA. Monday 10 April 1961

Born at Johannesburg, South Africa on 1 November 1935, Gary Player began playing golf at the age of 8 not long after his mother died of cancer, encouraged by his father Harry, who worked as a mining engineer. At 14 Gary Player played his first proper round of golf and parred the first three holes. Two years later, Player, nicknamed the Black Knight, predicted that one day he would become the world's best golfer.

Harry Player borrowed money to send his son abroad to compete in matches and learn additional skills. The young Player turned professional in 1953 and four years later joined the US PGA Tour. In 1958 he won the first of what would become two dozen PGA Tour triumphs and more than 160 tournament wins. In 1959 he won The Open at Muirfield and two years later became the first non-American to win the coveted green jacket by one stroke at 280 (68–69–68–74) from the amateur Charles Coe on 281 (72–71–69–69) and defending champion Arnold Palmer at 281 (68–69–73–71). On the final hole Player scored four from a bunker while Palmer took six for a double bogey from the same hole. Player once holed a difficult putt and a member of the crowd called out, 'Lucky shot, Gary.' The Black Knight responded, 'Yes it's strange, the more I practise the luckier I get.' (see 1978, page 181).

THE ONLY
PLAYER TO LOSE MASTERS
BECAUSE OF A HANDSHAKE
GARY PLAYER, US MASTERS, AUGUSTA NATIONAL GOLF CLUB, 2604
WASHINGTON ROAD, AUGUSTA, GEORGIA, USA. MONDAY 9 APRIL 1962

Looking forward to winning his second consecutive Masters title, Gary Player shook hands with a fan with a crushing grip. The handshake resulted in Player straining his right hand and having to seek medical attention. Playing the rest of the tournament with a bandage restricted his ability to hold the club properly and Player lost a play-off to Arnold Palmer.

THE FIRST
PROFESSIONAL WINNINGS
FOR JACK NICKLAUS
LOS ANGELES OPEN, RANCHO PARK GOLF COURSE, 10460 WEST PICO BOULEVARD, LOS ANGELES, CALIFORNIA, USA. JANUARY 1962

Jack Nicklaus was born at Columbus, Ohio, on 21 January 1940 and was stricken with polio as a child but made a full recovery. After breaking a bone in his left ankle playing volleyball, his father Charlie Nicklaus was told as part of his therapy to walk a few miles each day so he took up golf with Jack as his caddie at the Scioto Country Club. In school Nicklaus won six consecutive junior titles in Ohio, the first when he was just 12. He won the US Amateur Championship in September 1959 while a student at Ohio State University. He won it again in 1961 at Pebble Beach Golf Links, California, a course that opened in 1919. A year later, Jack Nicklaus won his first professional money, earning the princely sum of $33.33 at the Los Angeles Open when he finished in 50th place 21 strokes off the winner. The Golden Bear won the US Open in his first season as a pro and the following year on 21 July 1963 won the US PGA (pocketing $13,000).

THE FIRST
WIN IN ANY MAJOR CHAMPIONSHIP
BY A LEFT-HANDER
Bob Charles, The Open at Royal Lytham & St Annes Golf Club, Links Gate, Lytham St Annes, Lancashire, England. Friday 12 July 1963

New Zealander Bob Charles won The Open, beating Phil Rodgers in a play-off 140 to 148, the last decided over 36 holes. In 1909 Claud Felstead, a left-hander, had won the Australian Open.

THE ONLY
DIVISION ONE FOOTBALLER
KILLED BY LIGHTNING
ON A GOLF COURSE

**JOHN WHITE AT CREWS HILL GOLF COURSE, CATTLEGATE ROAD,
ENFIELD, MIDDLESEX, ENGLAND. TUESDAY 21 JULY 1964**

Tottenham Hotspur and Scotland international John White was born 28 April 1937 and began his career at Alloa Athletic. He moved to Falkirk before Bill Nicholson signed him for Spurs for £22,000 in October 1959. He became a mainstay of the Spurs side and they never finished lower than fourth with him in the team. Of the 15 games he missed while a Spurs player, the club won just one of them. He was on Crews Hill Golf Course, Enfield, in the summer of 1964 when a storm began. He took shelter under a tree and was instantly killed when struck by lightning. He was 27. A testimonial was arranged at White Hart Lane on 10 November 1964 between a Tottenham XI and a Scotland XI.

THE FIRST
BLACK PLAYER TO WIN A
PGA SPONSORED EVENT

PETE BROWN, WACO TURNER OPEN, BURNEYVILLE, OKLAHOMA, USA. 1964

The Waco Turner Open was held only four times, the last in 1964 when Pete Brown became the first black player to win a PGA Tour Event. He was born at Fort Gibson, Missouri, on 2 February 1935. Like many golfers, he began as a caddie and earned his PGA Tour card in 1963. In 1970 he won the Andy Williams-San Diego Open Invitational in a play-off with Tony Jacklin. Waco Turner, a millionaire Oklahoma oilman, had hoped to turn a 2,700-acre site into a major domestic and tourist resort with a hotel, restaurants, swimming pools, tennis courts and an airstrip built around three lakes. However, when the PGA stopped going to Burneyville after 1964 the development ran into money problems and it was never completed.

THE ONLY
PLAYER TO WIN
THE US OPEN
AND LOSE MONEY

GARY PLAYER, US OPEN AT BELLERIVE COUNTRY CLUB, 12925 LADUE
ROAD, ST LOUIS, MISSOURI, USA. MONDAY 21 JUNE 1965

Winners of the US Open usually make money. In 1965 Gary Player won
the competition beating Kel Nagle in a play-off 71 to 74 and the Black
Knight received a cheque for $26,000. The generous Player donated
$5,000 to cancer research, $20,000 to the US Golf Association to promote
golf among young players and still had to find $2,000 for his caddie
making a total of $27,000 – a grand more than Player had won.

THE LAST
OFFICIAL US PGA
WON BY SAM SNEAD

Greater Greensboro Open at Sedgefield Country Club, 3201 Forsyth
Drive, Greensboro, North Carolina, USA. 1965

Born on 27 May 1912 at Ashwood, Virginia, Sam Snead turned
professional in 1937 and won five competitions in his first year including
the Miami Open. In 1938 he also won the first of four Vardon trophies
for having the lowest average score on the PGA Tour. His other wins came
in 1949, 1950 and 1955. He won the Canadian Open in 1940 and 1941.
On 31 May 1942 at Seaview Country Club, New Jersey he won the US
PGA Championship for the first time, beating Jim Turnesa in the final by
2 and 1.

Surprisingly, in 1943 Snead did not win anything. In 1944 he won the
Richmond Open and Portland Open. Two years later, on 5 July 1946, he

won The Open at St Andrews and the World Championship of Golf in the same year. He won the green jacket at the US Masters on 10 April 1949 hitting 67 twice to finish on 282 despite high winds on the first two days of the tournament. In 1950 he won 11 tournaments.

Fifteen years later in 1965, he won the Greater Greensboro Open for the eighth and last time. It also made him the oldest player to win a PGA Tour event at almost 53. He had also won the Greater Greensboro Open in 1938, 1946, 1949, 1950, 1955, 1956 and 1960. The tournament has been known since 2007 as the Wyndham Championship when Wyndham Hotels & Resorts took over from DaimlerChrysler as main sponsor.

THE ONLY
COURSE WHOSE HOLES ARE NAMED AFTER TREASURE ISLAND

SPYGLASS HILL GOLF COURSE, SPYGLASS HILL AND STEVENSON DRIVE, PEBBLE BEACH, CALIFORNIA, USA. FRIDAY 11 MARCH 1966

Robert Louis Stevenson's tale of pirates and derring-do was first published in 1883. Stevenson wanted to call the book *The Sea Cook* and only latterly changed the title to the one that has made it a classic, *Treasure Island*. Rumour has it that Stevenson was spotted at Monterey seeking inspiration for his writings. The golf course logo is a one-legged pirate looking through a telescope. The holes have the following names: 1 Treasure Island; 2 Billy Bones; 3 The Black Spot; 4 Blind Pew; 5 Bird Rock; 6 Israel Hands; 7 Indian Village; 8 Signal Hill; 9 Captain Smollett; 10 Captain Flint; 11 Admiral Benbow; 12 Skeleton Island; 13 Tom Morgan; 14 Long John Silver; 15 Jim Hawkins; 16 Black Dog; 17 Ben Gunn and 18 Spyglass. The course took six years to plan and was designed by Robert Trent Jones Sr.

THE FIRST
PLAYER TO SUCCESSFULLY DEFEND
US MASTERS TITLE

**Jack Nicklaus, US Masters at Augusta National Golf Club, 2604
Washington Road, Augusta, Georgia, USA. Monday 11 April 1966**

There have been only three instances when the winner of the US Masters
has retained the title the following year. The first instance was in 1966
when Jack Nicklaus won beating Tommy Jacobs and Gay Brewer in a play-
off after all three hit 288. Nicklaus won the play-off by 70 to 72 to 78. It
was also the first Masters that was sold out prior to its start. In 1989 and
1990 Nick Faldo became the second man to retain the green jacket; the
third (in 2001 and 2002) was Tiger Woods.

THE ONLY
OPEN CHAMPION
KILLED IN AN
AEROPLANE CRASH

**TONY LEMA, LANSING COUNTRY CLUB, 18600 WENTWORTH
AVENUE, LANSING, ILLINOIS, USA. SUNDAY 24 JULY 1966**

'Champagne Tony' Lema was born at Oakland, California on 25 February
1934 and began playing golf at an early age but at 17 joined the US Marine
Corps and saw service in Korea. He was demobbed in 1955 and resumed
his interest in golf and two years later joined the PGA tour. He earned
his nickname by promising bubbly to journalists if he won the Orange
County Open Invitational in Costa Mesa, California in October 1962. He
duly won.

In 1963 he was beaten by one stroke by Jack Nicklaus at the Masters Tournament. On 10 July 1964 he won The Open Championship on the Old Course at St Andrews by five shots over Nicklaus.

In October 1963 at East Lake Country Club, Augusta, Georgia and 1965 at Royal Birkdale Golf Club, Southport he played for the USA in the Ryder Cup.

In 1966 he and his wife were flying in a chartered twin-engine Beechcraft Bonanza from the PGA Championship at Firestone Country Club in Akron, Ohio to the Little Buick Open in Lincolnshire, Illinois, south of Chicago, when the aeroplane ran out of fuel and crashed in a water hazard just short of the seventh green of Lansing Country Club. All aboard were killed.

THE ONLY
AMATEUR TO WIN THE US WOMEN'S OPEN

CATHERINE LACOSTE, US WOMEN'S OPEN AT HOT SPRINGS, VIRGINIA, USA. SUNDAY 2 JULY 1967

Catherine Lacoste, the daughter of French tennis player René Lacoste, was the first and so far only amateur and second overseas player to win the US Women's Open. Halfway through the tournament she was leading by five strokes and during the second half she increased her lead to seven strokes at one point, but faltered and in the end won by two strokes over Susie Maxwell and Beth Stone.

Catherine Lacoste also won the US and British women's amateur championships in 1969. Her mother, Simone Thion de la Chaume, became the first overseas player to win the British Women's Championship at Royal County Down, Newcastle, Northern Ireland, in 1927.

THE ONLY

GOLF BALL WITH WINGS

INVENTED BY ARTHUR PEDRICK, ENGLAND. MONDAY 18 JULY 1967

A golfing addict patented a new type of golf ball. The ball was fitted with hinged flaps that would fly out when the ball was struck to steady its flight. Pedrick said, 'If this can be achieved considerable benefit will have been added to the benefit of mankind.'

THE LAST

RYDER CUP TEAMS
CAPTAINED BY BEN HOGAN (USA) AND DAI REES (GB)

The Ryder Cup at Champions Golf Club, 13722 Champions Drive, Houston, Texas, USA. Friday 20–Sunday 22 October 1967.

In 1967 the 17th Ryder Cup came to the Lone Star state with both teams having non-playing captains – the Americans were led by Ben Hogan for the third and last time (previously 1947 and non-playing in 1949) while Dai Rees was in charge of the Britons for the fifth and as it also turned out the last time although this was the first time that he was non-playing.

At the pre-tournament dinner Rees gave a long and meandering speech about his team and their achievements. Hogan stood and asked that no one applaud until he had finished speaking. He introduced each team member by name but did not list their triumphs. With the entire team standing, he said, 'Ladies and gentlemen, the United States Ryder Cup Team – the finest golfers in the world.' Prior to the competition starting

Hogan had boasted to the press that he had brought 'the 12 best golfers in the world' to Houston.

It was no idle threat and America won by 23½ to 8½, the biggest win since the time the match was contested over six rounds. Britain won none of their eight fourballs. The US team was Julius Boros, Gene Littler, Gay Brewer, Bobby Nichols, Billy Casper, Arnold Palmer, Gardner Dickinson, Johnny Pott, Al Geiberger and Doug Sanders. On Dai Rees's team were Peter Alliss, Bernard Hunt, Hugh Boyle, Tony Jacklin, Neil Coles, Christy O'Connor Sr, Malcolm Gregson, Dave Thomas, Brian Huggett and George Will.

THE ONLY
PLAYER TO LOSE THE
US MASTERS FOR
MIS-SIGNING
HIS SCORE CARD

Roberto De Vicenzo, US Masters at Augusta National Golf Club, 2604 Washington Road, Augusta, Georgia, USA. Sunday 14 April 1968

Argentinean Roberto De Vincenzo hoped to celebrate his 45th birthday by winning his first US Masters. It was not to be – on the 17th hole in the final round De Vincenzo's playing partner Tommy Aaron marked the score card as a par 4 when in fact De Vincenzo had shot a birdie 3. The Argentinean did not notice the error and signed his card. The rules state that whatever is signed for is the accepted score so instead of a final round of 65 which would have tied him with Bob Goalby and forced a play-off for the sought-after green jacket, De Vincenzo was awarded 66 which left him in the runner-up spot. When he realized his costly error, he announced, 'What a stupid I am!'

THE FIRST
GOLFER TO EARN MORE THAN A MILLION DOLLARS

ARNOLD PALMER. TUESDAY 17 SEPTEMBER 1968

On 17 September 1968 Arnold Palmer passed the $1 million mark in career PGA earnings, ten years after he first won the US Masters and four years after he last won it (his last Major title in his homeland). Palmer's empire also including golf equipment, property, music, dry-cleaning, aftershaves, deodorants, soft drinks, sweets and power tools. In 1963, he had also become the first professional to earn more than $100,000 in official prize money in one calendar year when he earned $128,230 (£45,800). Perhaps Palmer's success had something to do with the comment reportedly made by an American television commentator at the 1960 US PGA tournament: 'One of the reasons Arnie is playing so well is that before every tee shot, his wife takes out his balls and kisses them.'

THE ONLY
CENTRALLY HEATED GOLF BALL

ENGLAND. MONDAY 31 MARCH 1969

An enterprising golfer realizing that golf balls travel further when they are warm invented a transparent sphere with a dark inside, which was supposed to absorb sunlight. To counter rainy and overcast days the ball had an additional refinement – inside was a heating element.

THE LAST
EUROPEAN TO DATE
TO WIN THE
US OPEN

TONY JACKLIN, US OPEN AT HAZELTINE NATIONAL GOLF CLUB, 1900
HAZELTINE BOULEVARD, CHASKA, MINNESOTA, USA. SUNDAY 21 JUNE 1970

The first British winner since Ted Ray in 1920, Jacklin led after every round and his seven-stroke winning margin was the biggest since Jim Barnes won by nine in 1921. Jacklin went round in 281 (71–70–70–70) but the following year failed to make the cut, the sixth title holder in nine years to fail to do so. The course at Hazeltine, the second longest to house a USGA championship, was criticised by Dave Hill, who came second, and was fined for his outburst.

THE ONLY
GAME OF GOLF
ON THE MOON

FRA MAURO COUNTRY CLUB, MOON. SATURDAY 6 FEBRUARY 1971

During the Apollo 14 mission 47-year-old Alan Bartlett Shepard Jr., the fifth man to walk on the moon, hit two balls using an improvised six-iron club made from an iron head and a makeshift shaft to play the only game of golf on the moon. His bulky spacesuit prevented him from taking a proper swing so he hit both balls one-handed. When the crew returned to Earth, they received the following telegram from the Royal & Ancient Golf Club in Scotland:

SHOTS IN SPACE

On 22 November 2006 Russian cosmonaut Mikhail Tyurin, 46, clung to a handrail on the side of the International Space Station 354 km (220 miles) above Earth. With a gold-plated six-iron strapped to his wrist, he hit a golf ball from a spring-loaded tee. 'All right. There it goes,' Tyurin said as the ball disappeared from sight and began orbiting Earth once every 90 minutes. Tyurin was 77 minutes behind schedule because he had to fix an overheating spacesuit and a jammed exterior hatch. To add to his woes, he could not maintain a stance to line up the ball and at one stage ended up upside down. 'The ball is the least of our concerns,' Tyurin said. 'It's me that is supposed to be positioned properly.' His 'caddie' for the shot was American astronaut Michael Lopez-Alegria who held on to his feet. Before he took aim, Tyurin was heard to complain, 'My feet are drifting away,' 'I'm afraid to move' and to Lopez-Alegria, 'Something's in my way... is it you?' The event was a publicity stunt for a Canadian golf club manufacturer who paid millions to Russian space agency Roskosmos, and claimed that the ball would keep orbiting the Earth for three years and would travel a billion miles. Holly Ridings of NASA, who has rather more experience in the field, said that it would orbit for two to three days, travelling a mere million miles before burning up in the Earth's atmosphere. Of greater concern for NASA was a worry that the ball would hit the space station. If so, NASA claimed, it could do so with the force of a 20-ton truck travelling at 160 k/ph (100 mph). Golf purists noted that as he hit the ball, Tyurin sliced it to the right.

'*Warmest congratulations to all of you on your great achievement and safe return. Please refer to the Rules of Golf section on etiquette, paragraph 6, quote – before leaving a bunker a player should carefully fill up all holes made by him therein – unquote.*'

In 1974 Shepard presented the club he had used to the United States Golf Association. He died on 21 July 1998 from leukaemia. He was 74.

THE FIRST

PLAYER TO WIN ALL FOUR MAJOR TOURNAMENTS TWICE

JACK NICKLAUS. SUNDAY 28 FEBRUARY 1971

When Jack Nicklaus beat Billy Casper by two shots to win the US PGA Championship on 28 February 1971, he became the first golfer to win all four Majors twice in a career.

Nicklaus won The Open in 1966 (at Muirfield) and 1970 (on the Old Course at St Andrews) and would win again in 1978 (again on the Old Course at St Andrews). He had won the US Open in 1962 (at Oakmont) and 1967 (at Baltusrol) and would win it again in 1972 (at Pebble Beach) and 1980 (again at Baltusrol).

His US Masters victories came in 1963, 1965 and 1966 and would come again in 1972, 1975 and 1986. He won the US PGA Championship in 1963 (at Dallas Athletic Country Club, Texas) and 1971 (at Oakland Hills Golf Club, Michigan), 1975 (at Firestone Country Club, Akron, Ohio) and 1980 (at Oak Hill Country Club, New York). By the end of 1971 the Golden Bear had won four more PGA tournaments including the Tournament of Champions by eight shots and the National Team Championship with Arnold Palmer by six shots. That year he made $244,490 in official PGA Tour earnings.

In total Nicklaus won an amazing 18 Majors, finishing second in a further 19. He also recorded an incredible 73 top-10 finishes in the 163 Major tournaments he played.

ANOTHER FACT ABOUT THIS PLAYER: Nicklaus is the ONLY player to win all four Major tournaments three times

THE ONLY
PLAYER TO SCORE CONSECUTIVE HOLES-IN-ONE IN A EUROPEAN TOUR EVENT

JOHN HUDSON, MARTINI INTERNATIONAL, ROYAL NORWICH
GOLF CLUB, DRAYTON ROAD, HELLESDEN, NORWICH, NORFOLK,
ENGLAND. FRIDAY 11 JUNE 1971

To get a hole-in-one once is an accomplishment most golfers never achieve. To get two is beyond their wildest dreams – to get two consecutively in a pro tournament is almost impossible. Yet that is what John Hudson did in the Martini International held at the Royal Norwich Golf Club between 10 and 12 June 1971. In his second round, Hudson holed the 195-yard (178 metres) at the 11th and 314-yard (287 metres) at the 12th holes with just one stroke each – five under par of two holes. He finished joint ninth and earned £160 from the tournament's total prize fund of £7,000.

THE ONLY
PLAYER TO WIN THE US PGA STANDING ON A CHAIR

GARY PLAYER AT OAKLAND HILLS COUNTRY CLUB, 3951 WEST
MAPLE ROAD, BLOOMFIELD HILLS, MICHIGAN, USA.
SUNDAY 6 AUGUST 1972

In the 1972 US PGA Championship Gary Player hit a bogey on both the 14th and 15th holes and then sliced his tee shot on the 16th. Things looked bad especially when he could not see the flag on the green to be able to judge his shot. Ever inventive, Player took a chair from the spectators and stood on it to arrange his approach shot. Taking a nine-iron the Black Knight hit his ball and saw it barely clear trees and a lake and then drop to within 4 ft (1 metre) of the hole. He holed for a birdie and went on to win his second US PGA title over Tommy Aaron and Jim Jamieson.

THE FIRST
TWO-PIECE GOLF BALL

Spalding. USA. 1972

The introduction by Spalding of the first two-piece ball, the Top-Flite, was the first successful major improvement on the ball invented by Coburn Haskell more than 70 years earlier.

THE ONLY
PLAYER TO GAIN A FREE SHOT FROM A BRA

Hale Irwin, Sea Pines Heritage Classic, Harbour Town Golf Links, Hilton Head, South Carolina, USA. September 1973

Playing in the Sea Pines Heritage Classic at Harbour Town Golf Links in South Carolina, Hale Irwin struck a ball that hit a female spectator in the chest. The ball then became lodged in her bra. For a time Irwin and the lady did not know how to proceed. A PGA official told the lady to take the ball out of her undergarment and drop it onto the green. Irwin was given a free drop. The bra must have brought Irwin luck for he won the competition on 16 September 1973 by five strokes, finishing 12 under par and taking home a cheque for $30,000.

THE FIRST

BLACK GOLFER
TO PLAY IN US MASTERS

LEE ELDER, THE US MASTERS AT AUGUSTA NATIONAL GOLF CLUB, 2604 WASHINGTON ROAD, AUGUSTA, GEORGIA, USA. THURSDAY 10-SUNDAY 13 APRIL 1975

Born on 14 July 1934 in Dallas, Texas, one of ten children, Robert Lee Elder began playing 18 holes of golf when he was 16. He was drafted into the army in 1959 and sent to Fort Lewis, Washington where he was able to play golf regularly. Demobbed in 1961, he joined the United Golf Association Tour for black players where he won 18 out of 22 competitions. He joined the PGA tour in 1968 and earned $38,000, ranking him 40th on the money list. Three years later, he won the Nigerian Open and then took part in the first mixed race tournament in South Africa, the South African PGA Championship in Johannesburg, as a guest of Gary Player. In 1974 he won the Monsanto Open beating Peter Oosterhuis, which allowed him entrance to the US Masters the following year, the first black player since its inception in 1934.

Elder was subjected to hate mail and threatening phone calls in the run-up to the tournament and he even went so far as to rent two houses to avoid his enemies. He also kept people with him whenever he went out to eat. Elder shot a 74 on day one and a 78 on day two and missed the cut. Jack Nicklaus won his fifth Masters, a victory that took him clear of Arnold Palmer's record of four. On 14–16 September 1979 Elder became the first black player to compete in the Ryder Cup.

THE FIRST
PLAYER TO WIN
THE US OPEN
WITHOUT EVER
BEING UNDER PAR

**LOU GRAHAM, THE US OPEN AT MEDINAH COUNTRY CLUB, 6N001
MEDINAH ROAD, MEDINAH, ILLINOIS, USA. SUNDAY 22 JUNE 1975**

Lou Graham won the US Open in 1975 in a play-off against John D. Mahaffey Jr. at Medina Country Club. Both players shot 287 over the four rounds – Graham's score was 74–72–68–73 while Mahaffey shot 73–71–72–71. The play-off was won by Graham 71 to 73. However, Graham was the first player to win the Major without ever being under par in a round. The feat was repeated when Corey Pavin won on 18 June 1995 at Shinnecock Hills Golf Club and Geoff Ogilvy won the 106th US Open on 18 June 2006 at Winged Foot Golf Club's West Course.

THE ONLY
PLAYERS STRUCK BY
LIGHTNING DURING A
PGA TOUR EVENT

Lee Trevino, Jerry Heard and Bobby Nichols, Western Open at Butler National Golf Club, 2616 York Rd, Oak Brook, Illinois, USA. Saturday 28 June 1975

The Mexican-born player was hit by lightning near the 13th hole in the second round of the Western Open at Butler National Golf Club. The lightning permanently damaged the flexibility and sensitivity of his lower back vertebrae. Jerry Heard and Bobby Nichols were struck during the same tournament. Trevino was leaning against his golf bag when he was hit and thrown into the air. He suffered a burned back. Heard was also thrown into the air and his groin was burned. Nichols, already with a metal plate in his head, was holding an eight-iron and was thrown backwards by the strike. All three players ended up in hospital and Trevino and Nichols pulled out of the competition. Heard played on and finished in third position. Trevino had to undergo several painful operations in an attempt to correct the damage to his back. On 19 August 1984, at the age of 44, he won the US PGA Trophy at Shoal Creek Country Club, Birmingham, Alabama.

Twenty-six people have been killed by lightning on golf courses since Trevino was struck but none were playing in PGA Tour events. During the June 1991 US Open at Hazeltine National Golf Club in Chaska, Minnesota, a spectator was killed after being struck by lightning.

THE ONLY
GOLFER TO KILL A GROUSE ON THE GLORIOUS TWELFTH...
WITH A GOLF BALL

Willie Fraser, Kingussie Golf Club, Gynack Road, Kingussie, Inverness-Shire, Scotland. Tuesday 12 August 1975

There are records of various animals being hit and injured or killed with golf balls – in 1994, a German farmer even tried to sue his local golf club for murdering 30 cows when they died after swallowing 3,000 golf balls – but the most appropriate animal death occurred on the first day of the grouse-hunting season in 1975 when 11-year-old Willie Fraser killed a grouse with his tee shot as he drove off.

THE FIRST

HOLE-IN-ONE
BY A LEFT-HANDER
AT THE OPEN

**PETER DAWSON, THE OPEN AT ROYAL BIRKDALE GOLF CLUB,
WATERLOO ROAD, SOUTHPORT, MERSEYSIDE, ENGLAND.
SATURDAY 10 JULY 1976**

In the long, hot summer of 1976 in which Johnny Miller won The Open from Severiano Ballesteros, Peter Dawson holed-in-one on the fourth, the first such feat by a southpaw.

ALSO ON THAT OCCASION: Such was the heat that at one point part of the course caught fire, the FIRST time at The Open that this happened

THE FIRST

PROFESSIONAL PLAYER
TO BREAK 60
ON THE US PGA TOUR

**AL GEIBERGER, DANNY THOMAS MEMPHIS CLASSIC, SOUTH
COURSE AT COLONIAL COUNTRY CLUB, 2736 COUNTRYWOOD
PARKWAY, CORDOVA, TENNESSEE, USA. FRIDAY 10 JUNE 1977**

The first professional golfer to play a round in fewer than 60 strokes on an official PGA Tour tournament was 39-year-old Al Geiberger in his second round at the Danny Thomas Memphis Classic. In the tournament preferred lies were in use so Geiberger could lift, clean and place his ball. His score consisted of 11 birdies, one eagle and 23 putts and he finished

13 under par on the 7,249-yard (6,628 metres) course. In 1991 Chip Beck equalled Geiberger's score in the third round of the 1991 Las Vegas Invitational at Sunrise Golf Club. He could not, however, emulate Geiberger by winning and Beck finished in third place.

THE ONLY
PLAYER TO PLAY
IN THE US OPEN
UNDER THREAT OF DEATH

HUBERT GREEN, US OPEN AT SOUTHERN HILLS COUNTRY CLUB, 2636 EAST 61ST STREET, TULSA, OKLAHOMA, USA. SUNDAY 19 JUNE 1977

In 1977 Hubert Green was leading the US Open when police learned via a telephone call of a threat to his life. They informed the tournament authorities who told the player during the last round and gave him the chance to withdraw. Green decided to play on and indeed won the championship by one stroke over Lou Graham, holing from under 1 yard (0.9 metres) .

THE FIRST
PLAYER TO WIN
THE OPEN WITH A
SCORE UNDER 270

TOM WATSON, THE OPEN, AILSA COURSE AT TURNBERRY, MAIDENS ROAD, AYRSHIRE, SCOTLAND. SATURDAY 9 JULY 1977

From the time The Open was changed to a 72-hole competition, scores in the 290s and 300s were not unusual (J. H. Taylor won in 1894 with a score of 326 and in 1926 Bobby Jones triumphed with 291). With the passage of time the scores began to come down but not by much. On 3

July 1959 Gary Player won with a score of 284 at Muirfield. On 10 July 1976 Johnny Miller won at Royal Birkdale with 279. The following year Tom Watson smashed that score out of sight when he went round Turnberry in just 268 strokes (68–70–65–65). The runner-up was Jack Nicklaus with 269.

The contest became known as the Duel in the Sun. Both men went into the final round three shots ahead of the rest of the field. Nicklaus and Watson then tied through the 16th hole. At the par five 17th hole, Nicklaus missed a short birdie putt to level again with Watson who had birdied. At the last, par-four hole Nicklaus hit his ball into the rough but managed to recover sufficiently to hole a lengthy birdie putt. However, Watson sank his short birdie putt to take the title – his second of what would be five Opens.

However, since then only three other players have won with a score of under 270: Greg Norman with 267 on 18 July 1993, Nick Price 268 on 17 July 1994 (also at Turnberry) and Tiger Woods on 23 July 2000 with 269. Woods came close again on 23 July 2006 when he went round in 270.

THE FIRST
SUDDEN-DEATH PLAY-OFF IN A
MAJOR CHAMPIONSHIP

US PGA Championship at Pebble Beach Golf Links, 1700 17 Mile Drive, Pebble Beach, California, USA. Sunday 14 August 1977

The first sudden death was used for the US PGA Championship in 1977. Wadkins was playing Gene Littler, who led from the first round. The last round began with Wadkins six shots behind Littler. As they approached the final nine holes Wadkins had not improved by much – he was still five behind, despite two front-nine eagles. Then things moved in Wadkins's favour as Littler bogeyed five of the first six holes off the remaining nine. Wadkins pulled level with Littler, with his only birdie of the day at the 18th and then finished the play-off with a 2 yard (1.8 metre) par putt on the third extra hole to win $45,000. Two years later, on 15 April 1979 a sudden-death play-off decided the US Masters in favour of Fuzzy Zoeller who became the first golfer to win the coveted green jacket in his inaugural Masters appearance since Gene Sarazen in 1935.

THE ONLY

OSCAR WINNER

TO DIE ON A GOLF COURSE

BING CROSBY, LA MORALEJA GOLF CLUB, MARQUESA VIUDA DE ALDAMA, 50, ALCOBENDAS, MADRID, SPAIN. FRIDAY 14 OCTOBER 1977

Crosby was the first celebrity to sponsor his own tournament on the professional circuit in America. The first Bing Crosby tournament, the National Pro-Amateur Golf Championship was held at Rancho Santa Fe Golf Club in Rancho Santa Fe, California in 1937. It was won by Sam Snead who took home a cheque for $500. From 1953 to 1955 it was known as the Bing Crosby Pro-Am Invitational; from 1956 to 1958 the Bing Crosby National Pro-Am Golf Championship; from 1959 to 3 February 1985 the Bing Crosby National Pro-Am and from 2 February 1986 it has been the AT&T Pebble Beach National Pro-Am.

After a successful tour of England in 1977 – his last public performance was at the Brighton Centre two days before his death – Bing Crosby set off for Spain on 13 October to play golf and do some hunting. On arrival he took to the course and scored 92. The Old Groaner had been told by a doctor to play no more than nine holes but he ignored the advice. The next day he was back on the course playing with then-Spanish champion Manuel Pinero against another Spanish champion Valentin Barrios and Cesar de Zulueta, the president of La Moraleja Golf Club. Crosby was in high spirits, singing and whistling and telling jokes.

CHIP OFF THE OLD BLOCK

In 1981 Nathaniel Crosby, Bing's son, won the US Amateur Championship at Olympic Club, San Francisco, California. It was almost a home competition for Crosby – the course was just a few miles from the Crosby family home at Hillsborough. Crosby beat Brian Lindley on the 37th, the first final to go to extra holes since 1956.

On the 15th hole the others noticed that the Old Groaner was favouring his left arm. Crosby insisted that he was all right and the game continued. At just after 6 pm having just completed the 18th hole and won the match, he suffered a massive heart attack. He was dead before the ambulance could get to Madrid's Red Cross Hospital. He was 74. He said he wanted his epitaph to read 'He was an average guy who could carry a tune.'

In his will, Crosby stated that none of his sons could use the trust fund he had set up for them until they reached 65. Crosby's son Gary wrote a book after his father's death saying that Bing had tortured him. His old friend Bob Hope stated, 'Bing used to sing to me too but I didn't feel I had to write a book about it.'

BING CROSBY WAS ALSO: The **FIRST** Oscar winner to sponsor a pro-am tournament

THE ONLY
SPONSORSHIP DEAL
PAID IN BURGERS
Howard Twitty. 1977

In today's game, players can receive millions of dollars in lucrative sponsorship deals for sporting a manufacturer's logo on their clothes or using their equipment on or off the course. Things have not always been so complicated. In 1977 Howard Twitty, who was born in Phoenix, Arizona on 15 January

---

NOT PUTTING A FOOT WRONG

Following surgery on his foot, Howard Twitty was forced to miss part of the 1996 season. As a result he now plays in specially adapted sandals with added spikes.

1949, signed a deal with Burger King. In exchange for putting the company logo on his golf bag, Burger King gave him 500 Whoppers.

THE ONLY

FATHER AND SON TO PLAY IN THE RYDER CUP AND WALKER CUP

CLAYTON HEAFNER, RYDER CUP AT GANTON GOLF CLUB, STATION ROAD, SCARBOROUGH, YORKSHIRE, ENGLAND. FRIDAY 16–SATURDAY 17 SEPTEMBER 1949; AND VANCE HEAFNER, WALKER CUP AT SHINNECOCK HILLS, 200 TUCKAHOE ROAD, SOUTHAMPTON, LONG ISLAND, NEW YORK, USA. 1977

Clayton Heafner (1914–1960) was a man with a temper – he once walked off a course at the first tee after the announcer mispronounced his name. He represented the USA in the Ryder Cup in 1949 when he beat Dick Burton 3 and 2. Two years later, he was back in the team on the only occasion the tournament was held at Pinehurst Resort. He halved his match with Fred Daly as the United States won 9½ to 2½ on 2–4 November 1951. His son Vance was just six when he died on New Year's Eve 1960. Vance Heafner played in 266 events on the US PGA Tour between 1978 and 1988, and he made the cut 157 times. He represented his country in the Walker Cup in 1977 when the US beat Great Britain and Northern Ireland 16 to 8.

THE LAST

MAJOR
TOURNAMENT WIN BY
GARY PLAYER

THE US MASTERS AT AUGUSTA NATIONAL GOLF CLUB, 2604 WASHINGTON
ROAD, AUGUSTA, GEORGIA, USA. THURSDAY 6–SUNDAY 9 APRIL 1978

Born at Johannesburg in Transvaal, Player was the first overseas golfer to win
the US Masters so it was fitting that the tournament was also his last Major
win. He also won the US Masters on 14 April 1974. In his last winning round
he started seven strokes behind the leader Hubert Green. But Player was
resilient and had seven birdies in the last 10 holes to equal the Augusta record
of 64. Then he waited for Rod Funseth, Green and Tom Watson to make
mistakes, which they did and so he won his third US Masters. The Black
Knight's victory at the South African PGA Championship at the Wanderers,
Johannesburg on 17 January 1982 was the 123rd of his career.

THE ONLY

BRITISH CABINET MINISTER
TO HAVE BEEN CAPTAIN OF THE
ROYAL & ANCIENT

WILLIAM WHITELAW, SECRETARY OF STATE FOR THE HOME
DEPARTMENT, FRIDAY 4 MAY 1979

The Secretary of State for the Home Office in Margaret Thatcher's first
Cabinet, Willie Whitelaw had, ten years earlier, been the captain of the
Royal & Ancient. Before that, Whitelaw, the man of whom Mrs Thatcher
said, 'Every prime minister needs a Willie', was a Blue at Cambridge.

THE FIRST
PROFESSIONAL PLAYER
TO SHOOT BELOW HIS AGE
ON A US PGA TOUR

SAM SNEAD, QUAD CITIES OPEN, COAL CITY, ILLINOIS, USA. SUNDAY 22 JULY 1979

The first professional golfer to play below his age was 67-year-old Sam Snead who shot a 66 on the fourth day of the Quad Cities Open Championship. His final score was 277 (70–67–74–66).

THE FIRST
PGA GRAND SLAM
OF GOLF

EAST COURSE, OAK HILL COUNTRY CLUB, 346 KILBOURN ROAD, ROCHESTER, NEW YORK, USA. TUESDAY 7 AUGUST 1979

The most prestigious golf tournament, it is contested by the four winners of the Major championships: The Open, the US Open, the US Masters and US PGA Championship. Held in the close season, it is arranged by the PGA of America but the money is not included on the list of the PGA Tour. From its inaugural event in 1979 until 1990 it was a one-day, 18-hole strokeplay competition.

That changed in 1991 when it became a two-day 36-hole strokeplay competition (apart from 1998 and 1999). If for any reason a player does not wish to compete or cannot (for example, in October 2008 Tiger Woods did not participate because he had undergone an operation on his knee) or if he wins more than one of the Majors, then the PGA turns to a former winner of a Major with the best result in that year's tournaments.

The first competitors were John Mahaffey (winner of the US PGA), Jack Nicklaus (winner of The Open), Andy North (US Open winner) and Gary Player (the victor in US Masters). The result, uniquely, was two ties, with Andy North and Gary Player scoring 73 and sharing the $12,000 Steuben Trophy and Mahaffey and Nicklaus hitting 77 on the par-70, 6,974-yard (6,377 metres) course. The event was arranged to benefit the PGA's Junior Golf Foundation and fans paid $25 or $30 to watch and another $100 to attend an evening awards presentation featuring the contestants, President Gerald Ford, singer Pat Boone and comedian Foster Brooks and sports presenter Chris Schenkel. When expenses were taken out of the equation, the Junior Golf Foundation received more than $75,000.

THE FIRST
METAL WOODS
TaylorMade, Carlsbad, California, USA. 1979

Gary Adams went to the 1979 PGA Merchandise Show where he showed off his new invention – the metal wood. His company, TaylorMade, began making drivers and other woods out of metal. Two years later, Ron Streck became the first winner of a professional tournament (Houston Open) with a metal wood. Gary Adams died of cancer on 2 January 2000, aged 56.

THE LAST
BRITISH PGA MATCHPLAY CHAMPIONSHIP
BRITISH PGA MATCHPLAY CHAMPIONSHIP AT FULFORD GOLF CLUB, YORK, ENGLAND. 1979

The British PGA Matchplay Championship began in 1903 and until 1969 was sponsored by the *News of the World*. The purse for the tournament was one of the largest in the game. In 1907, the fifth competition, the semi-finalists were Ted Ray and the 'Great Triumvirate' of James Braid, Harry Vardon and J. H. Taylor. Braid went on to win the championship, which was held at Sunningdale.

Participants tended to be from Commonwealth countries, and Australia's Peter Thomson won it four times, a record he shares with Dai Rees and James Braid. In 1949 the eight American players from the Ryder Cup stayed to play in the tournament. The most successful that year was Lloyd Mangrum who made it to the semi-finals. In 1955 with the establishment of the British PGA Championship (at strokeplay), the matchplay variation became less and less popular. From 1972 until 1979 it counted in the money listings of the European tour. The last winner was Irishman Des Smyth, who beat Nick Price in the final.

THE FIRST
CONTINENTAL EUROPEAN
TO WIN US MASTERS

SEVERIANO BALLESTEROS, US MASTERS AT AUGUSTA NATIONAL
GOLF CLUB, 2604 WASHINGTON ROAD, AUGUSTA, GEORGIA, USA.
SUNDAY 13 APRIL 1980

At just 23 Spaniard Severiano Ballesteros became the first Continental European and the youngest player to win the green jacket at the US Masters, winning by four strokes over Gibby Gilbert and Jack Newton. He went round in 275 (66–69–68–72) a total of 13 under par. Ballesteros led or was tied for the lead on each of the four rounds, and had 23 birdies, which was a record for a winner at that time. The US Masters was one of four PGA Tour events that Ballesteros won in 1980. He won the green jacket again in 1983.

THE ONLY

PLAYER TO WIN THE US OPEN

IN THREE DIFFERENT DECADES

Jack Nicklaus, US Open at Oakmont Country Club, 1233 Hulton Road, Oakmont, Pennsylvania, USA. Saturday 17 June 1962; Pebble Beach Golf Links, 1700 17 Mile Drive, Pebble Beach, California, USA. Sunday 18 June 1972; Baltusrol Golf Club, 201 Shunpike Road, Springfield Township, Union County, New Jersey, USA. Sunday 15 June 1980

Although other golfers have won the US Open on more than one occasion, the Golden Bear is the only player to have won the tournament in three different decades. In 1962 he beat Arnold Palmer in a play-off after both men scored 283. Ten years and one day later, he beat Bruce Crampton by three strokes (290 to 293) and then in 1980 he beat Isao Aoki by two strokes (272 to 274). Nicklaus also won a second time in the 1960s, winning at Baltusrol Golf Club on 18 June 1967, beating Arnold Palmer again, albeit on this occasion by a more convincing four strokes.

THE ONLY

PROFESSIONAL PLAYER TO TRAVEL TO A TOURNAMENT ON TRANSPORT SUPPLIED BY HELL'S ANGELS

GARY PLAYER, WORLD SERIES OF GOLF AT FIRESTONE COUNTRY CLUB, AKRON, OHIO, USA. 1980

On his way to the World Series of Golf, Gary Player's courtesy car became caught in a traffic jam. Player was due to tee off in the third round but the traffic was so heavy that he was still 3 miles (5 km) from the course with just 25 minutes before he was due to be called. Player drove on to the hard shoulder where he abandoned his car and prepared to run the remainder of the route. As he built up pace, he spotted a group of Hell's Angels aboard their powerful Harley Davidsons.

Player waved them down and offered to pay for the petrol for all of their motorbikes if one of them would give him a lift to the Firestone Country Club. They agreed and Player got on to a motorbike for the first time in his life. He clung on for dear life as the biker wound his way through the cars and to the golf course where he deposited the diminutive South African outside the changing rooms. The two men agreed on a fee of $20. Player said to a fellow competitor after he had shot a 3 under par 69, 'Imagine – only $20. Why, had he not had long, greasy hair and beard, I could have kissed him.'

THE FIRST
PLAYER TO EARN PRIZE MONEY OF $500,000 IN ONE SEASON
Tom Watson. 1980

Thomas Sturges Watson was born at Kansas City, Missouri on 4 September 1949. He began playing professionally in 1971 after graduating from Stanford University with a degree in psychology. It took him some time to establish himself as he had an early reputation as a player who fluffed it when the stakes were high. In 1974 he won the Western Open Championship, the first of his 39 PGA Tour wins. In 1975 he did not play well at either the US Masters or US Open competitions and so when he arrived at Carnoustie for The Open, he was not among the favoured players.

However, Watson had formed a steely determination and on 12 July he took The Open title with a score of 279, beating Jack Newton of Australia in a play-off 71 to 72. It was the first of Watson's eight Majors and five

Opens. In 1976 he had a comparatively poor season but in 1977 he won the US Masters on 10 April and on 9 July at Turnberry he won his second Open. In 1978 he won five PGA Tour titles. Two years later, in 1980, he became the first player to earn prize money of $500,000 in one season when he took home $530,808. He won seven PGA titles and on 20 July 1980 his third Open.

THE FIRST
PROFESSIONAL PLAYER
TO DIVE INTO A WATER HAZARD
TO CELEBRATE A VICTORY

JERRY PATE. DANNY THOMAS MEMPHIS CLASSIC AT COLONIAL COUNTRY CLUB, SOUTH COURSE, 2736 COUNTRYWOOD PARKWAY, CORDOVA, TENNESSEE, USA. SUNDAY 28 JUNE 1981

Players usually do their utmost to avoid water hazards but not so Jerry Pate. He promised that he would 'bathe in victory' if he won the 1981 Danny Thomas Memphis Classic. When he sank the final putt to win, he kept his word and dived fully dressed into a lake near the 18th hole. The $54,000 prize money probably helped with his dry-cleaning bill.

THE FIRST
WOMAN TO EARN CAREER
PRIZE MONEY OF $1 MILLION

KATHY WHITWORTH. 1981

Kathy Whitworth was born at Monahans, Texas on 27 September 1939 and started playing golf at 15 when her grandfather gifted her a set of clubs. At 17 she won the first of two consecutive New Mexico State Amateur titles. Turning pro did not bring immediate success – in 26 events she made less than $1,300 and considered giving up. Buoyed by other golfers she tried again and began winning. 'When I won eight tournaments in 1963, I was living on a high. I got in a winning syndrome. I played really well and it came easily. You don't think you're that great, but you're in the groove with good concentration. Nothing bothers you.'

In 1966 she won the Vare Trophy and was named as the inaugural LPGA Player of the year. In 1975 she was inducted into the LPGA Hall of Fame but then her game worsened and only the thought of earning $1 million kept her going. When she came third in the US Women's Open at La Grange, Illinois, on 26 July 1981 she took the amount of money that she had won in her career above the million dollar mark. In comparison, by the end of 1981, some 32 men had won more than a $1 million in prize money. When she retired she had won 88 competitions. She said:

I don't think about the legacy of 88 tournaments – I did it because I wanted to win, not to set a record or a goal that no one else could surpass. I'm not some great oddity. I was just fortunate to be so successful. What I did in being a better player does not make me a better person. When I'm asked how I would like to be remembered, I feel that if people remember me at all, it will be good enough.

THE FIRST

GOLF TOURNAMENT TO OFFER A $1 MILLION PURSE

SUN CITY, BOPHUTHATSWANA, SOUTH AFRICA. THURSDAY 31 DECEMBER 1981–SUNDAY 3 JANUARY 1982

The first golf competition with prize money of $1 million was organized by Sol Kerzner, the owner of the Sun City resort complex in South Africa. Johnny Miller won the first tournament held at Sun City and a $500,000 first prize.

THE FIRST

SKINS GAME

**DESERT HIGHLANDS COUNTRY CLUB, 10040 EAST HAPPY
VALLEY ROAD, SCOTTSDALE, ARIZONA, USA. 1983**

The Skins Game was invented by Gary Frank and Don Ohlmeyer in 1983. The first participants were Arnold Palmer, Gary Player, Jack Nicklaus and Tom Watson. The Black Knight won the inaugural competition and boosted his bank balance by $170,000. The idea was to hold a two-day, 18-hole matchplay competition that was televised. Four golfers are invited to participate each year and the winner of each hole earns a sum of money for that hole. If the hole is halved, the money is added to that of the next hole. Fuzzy Zoeller won in 1985 and retained his title in 1986 to become the first two-time winner. Payne Stewart won in 1991, 1992 and 1993 to become the first three-time winner and the only player to win three times consecutively.

THE FIRST

GERMAN TO WIN A
MAJOR CHAMPIONSHIP

Bernhard Langer, US Masters at Augusta National Golf Club, 2604 Washington Road, Augusta, Georgia, USA. Sunday 14 April 1985

In 1980 Langer won the Dunlop Masters at St Pierre but five years later, playing in his third US Masters, Langer became the third international player to win the tournament with weekend rounds of 68 and 68. Curtis Strange, Severiano Ballesteros and Raymond Floyd all tied for second place, two strokes behind the champion. Langer had also been the first German to win the German Open triumphing in 1981, 70 years after its inauguration. That same year playing in the Benson & Hedges Tournament at Fulford, York, he managed to hit his second shot on the 17th into a tree. He simply climbed into the tree and hit the ball onto the green.

THE FIRST
STREAKER
AT THE OPEN

THE OPEN AT THE ROYAL ST GEORGE'S GOLF CLUB, SANDWICH, KENT, ENGLAND. JULY 1985

Streaking began in the 1970s when people began taking their clothes off at public events and running around. The craze even produced a novelty hit number one record 'The Streak' by Ray Stevens in 1974. The first streaker to hit The Open was a man in 1985 at Sandwich. He approached Peter Jacobsen on the 18th green and rather than letting him pass by, the golfer tackled him. Jacobsen remembered:

'As the guy ran by us, I just got down low and hit him hard. I hit him about waist high and turned my head to the side because I didn't want to get a mouthful of parsley, if you know what I mean. He was a little guy and he was little in another area, too, so I stood up after the tackle and I pointed out to the crowd. I held my fingers about an inch apart, and I said, "He has a tap-in," since they didn't have as close-up a view as I did of his endowment. Then the Bobbies were on him, and it all happened so quickly. I made bogey on that hole, and I don't think anyone got a bigger ovation in Open history for making bogey on the 18th hole.'

Jacobsen tied in 11th place, six above par in The Open as Sandy Lyle won the competition. Twelve years later, in July 1997, at Royal Troon, a beautiful blonde called Nikki Moffat stripped to her black thong to reveal that her body as well as her face was painted in tiger stripes (she even had tiger ears) in her own unique tribute to Tiger Woods.

THE FIRST
FORMALLY RECOGNIZED
MEN'S PLAYING RANKINGS
THE SONY RANKINGS SYSTEM. TUESDAY 8 APRIL 1986

The first rankings for male golfers were introduced in April 1986 and was then sponsored by the Japanese electronics giant Sony. The first player ranked at number one was the 1985 US Masters Champion Bernhard Langer. It is now called the Official World Golf Rankings.

THE LAST

MAJOR TOURNAMENT
WIN BY JACK NICKLAUS

US Masters at Augusta National Golf Club, 2604 Washington Road, Augusta, Georgia, USA. Thursday 10–Sunday 13 April 1986

Jack Nicklaus won his 18th and last Major competition when he won his sixth US Masters – and thus, at 46, became the oldest Masters winner in history. Nicklaus had been written off by many before the tournament started. Tom McCollister, writing in the *Atlanta Journal-Constitution*, said that Nicklaus was 'done, washed up, through', which inspired the golfer. He said later, 'I kept thinking all week, "Through, washed up, huh?" I sizzled for a while. But then I said to myself, "I'm not going to quit now, playing the way I'm playing. I've played too well, too long to let a shorter period of bad golf be my last."' Nicklaus then posted a six-under par 30 on the back nine at Augusta for a final round of seven-under par 65. The Golden Bear made a victory-sealing par-4 at the 72nd hole and played the last ten holes seven under par with six birdies and an eagle.

THE ONLY

PLAYER TO LEAVE A
PROFESSIONAL TOURNAMENT
AFTER RUNNING OUT OF BALLS

BILL KRATZERT, ANHEUSER-BUSCH GOLF CLASSIC, RIVER COURSE AT KINGSMILL GOLF CLUB, 1010 KINGSMILL ROAD, WILLIAMSBURG, VIRGINIA, USA. JULY 1986

Before setting off for the course, most golfers check their golf bag to make sure that they have the requisite number of clubs (no more than 14 – as

Ian Woosnam found to his cost, see page 32) and a copious supply of golf balls. In the hot Virginia summer of 1986 Bill Kratzert took part in the Anheuser-Busch Golf Classic but his caddie, to lighten the load, took out some balls. As he played Kratzert lost three balls and going to his bag found no more. He had no choice but to withdraw from the competition.

THE ONLY
PLAYER DISQUALIFIED FOR PROTECTING HIS TROUSERS

CRAIG STADLER. ANDY WILLIAMS SAN DIEGO OPEN AT TORREY PINES GOLF COURSE, 11480 NORTH TORREY PINES ROAD, LA JOLLA, CALIFORNIA, USA. SATURDAY 14 FEBRUARY 1987

The Walrus teed up on the 14th hole and drove but was dismayed to see his shot land under a pine tree at Torrey Pines. To play the ball where it lay, he had to get on his hands and knees but unwilling to get mud on his golf trousers Stadler laid a towel down and knelt on it before striking the ball.

Stadler completed his round and signed his scorecard. That evening scores of television viewers rang in to complain that under Rule 13.3 the Walrus had technically 'built a stance', which is illegal. As he had already signed his card and not added a two-point penalty, he had submitted a score lower than the reality and was thus disqualified. Some years later, Stadler was invited back to the course and offered a chainsaw to cut down the offending tree. He did so with gusto.

THE ONLY
AIR FORCE DESTROYED BY A GOLF BALL

BENIN. 1987

The west African republic of Benin did not have much in the way of facilities for golfers so keen player Mathieu Boya practised his drives next to the national air force base. One day he hit a fierce shot that hit a seagull flying over the base, knocking it unconscious. The bird dropped into The Open cockpit of a plane taxiing on the runway. The pilot lost control and smashed into four stationary Mirage III jets writing off all five planes at a cost of $40 million. Boya was sent to prison and told that he would be released when he was able to repay the damages.

THE ONLY
GOLF HOLE TO STRADDLE TWO COUNTRIES

SIXTH HOLE, GREEN ZONE GOLF CLUB, NÄRÄNTIE, 95400 TORNIO, FINLAND. 1987

Opened in 1987, the Green Zone or Tornio Golf Club has nine holes in Finland and nine in Sweden. The 132-yard (120 metres), par 3 sixth hole has its tee in Sweden while the green rests in Finland. It is also divided by two time zones. Due to its location, it is possible to play 24 hours a day during the golf season because the sun never sets between June and August. Passports are not required to play the course.

THE FIRST
BRITISH PLAYER TO WIN US MASTERS

Sandy Lyle, US Masters at Augusta National Golf Club, 2604 Washington Road, Augusta, Georgia, USA. Saturday 10 April 1988

Alexander 'Sandy' Lyle took his victory down to the wire. He swept his approach shot to the last green out of a fairway bunker to within 5 yards (4.5 metres) and sank the resulting birdie putt for a one-shot victory over Mark Calcavecchia. It was the fourth time a birdie on the final hole had won the US Masters and also the first time it had happened in ten years.

THE ONLY

PRO PLAYER TO WIN A COW

IAN BAKER-FINCH. BRIDGESTONE ASO OPEN CHAMPIONSHIP, ASO GOLF CLUB, KUMAMOTO, JAPAN. 1988

When Ian Baker-Finch became the third non-Japanese to win the Bridgestone Aso Open in 1988 (it started in 1977 with an unofficial tournament) he was surprised to discover that among his prize purse was a cow. Aso is a large dairy produce centre in Japan. Baker-Finch sold the cow back to the tournament's sponsors.

THE ONLY

PLAYER DISQUALIFIED FOR ANSWERING THE CALL OF NATURE

FRED ROWLAND. THE AMATEUR CHAMPIONSHIP AT ROYAL PORTHCAWL GOLF CLUB, REST BAY, PORTHCAWL, MID GLAMORGAN, WALES. 1988

When Fred Rowland entered the Amateur Championship in 1988 he probably did not expect to be disqualified before he had even teed off. That, however, is the fate that befell him. He prepared to tee off when he suddenly had an urgent need to answer the call of nature. He disappeared into a Portaloo to complete his business and, in doing so, missed the call of his name by the announcer. When he returned to the tee, he discovered that his playing partner had left without him and Rowland was told that since he was not present, he had been thrown out of the competition.

THE FIRST
PLAYER TO EARN
PRIZE MONEY OF $1 MILLION IN ONE SEASON
CURTIS STRANGE. 1988

In 1988 Curtis Strange beat Nick Faldo in a play-off to win his first Major title, the US Open. He finished the season by winning the Nabisco Championships at Pebble Beach and a cheque for $360,000 that brought his seasonal earnings to $1,147,644 – the first player to break the seven-figure sum in the same season.

THE FIRST
SOLHEIM CUP
LAKE NONA GOLF AND COUNTRY CLUB, 9801 LAKE NONA ROAD, ORLANDO, FLORIDA, USA. FRIDAY 16-SUNDAY 18 NOVEMBER 1990

The Solheim Cup is contested between professional lady golfers from the USA and Europe. The trophy was donated by Karsten Solheim and his wife Louise. Karsten Solheim, a Norwegian-born American aeroplane designer was the founder of the Ping Company that created the most popular putter of all time. The Solheim Cup is played biennially over three days. The first was won by the USA with a score of $11\frac{1}{2}$ to $4\frac{1}{2}$.

THE ONLY
COMPETITION WITH
TOPLESS CADDIES
FOREST CREEK GOLF COURSE, 99 TWIN RIDGE PARKWAY, ROUND ROCK, TEXAS, USA. 1990

Nightclubs in Austin, Texas sponsored a golf tournament from 1990 until 1992 at the Forest Creek Golf Course. The 'caddies' were topless go-go dancers from those clubs, and as well as looking after the clubs, they drove golf carts and delivered drinks and other refreshments to the participants. In July 2000 David Calhoun, the manager of the Beaver Creek Golf Links at Oakland, Michigan took out a full-page newspaper advertisement to apologise to anyone who had been upset by the sight of 20 topless and naked women at his course. Mr Calhoun said, 'Maybe my judgment wasn't the best in the world,' when he rented the course to Mannequins, a Detroit topless bar, for a private event. He said that the women had broken their promises to keep their bikinis on.

THE ONLY
HEIR PRESUMPTIVE'S SKULL
TO BE FRACTURED
BY A GOLF CLUB

Prince William, Ludgrove Preparatory School, Ludgrove, Wokingham, Berkshire, England. Monday 3 June 1991

In September 1990 Prince William, the elder son of the Prince of Wales, was sent to Ludgrove Preparatory School. Nine months later, William and other pupils were practising their golf swings during the lunch break when another boy swung his club rather too enthusiastically and hit the future king of England on the head. William, bleeding but conscious, was taken to the Royal Berkshire Hospital where doctors found that he had a depressed skull fracture just above the eye. He was transferred to Great Ormond Street Hospital where neurosurgeon Richard Hayward conducted a 70-minute operation on the injury. The wound needed 24 stitches to close. William spent two days in hospital before he was released.

THE ONLY
PLAYER TO BREAK HIS LEG
DURING THE OPEN

Richard Boxall, The Open at Royal Birkdale Golf Club, Waterloo Road, Southport, Merseyside, England. Saturday 20 July 1991

Richard Boxall had high hopes in the 1991 Open as he went to tee off at the ninth in the third round. He hit rounds of 71 and 69. Boxall was just three shots behind the championship leader when disaster struck and he managed to fracture his left leg, thus putting himself out of the running and the competition.

Such was the discomfort felt by Boxall that he was unable to watch a recording of the incident until 2007. 'It made me feel ill looking at it,' he recalled. 'What a noise my leg made when it snapped.' Boxall had had twinges of pain in his left leg at the start of the competition but believed it was just nerves. 'I practised with Gary Player and every time I went for something quickly I had pain in my left ankle. After the second round I had a funny feeling down my leg and spoke to Chubby Chandler, my manager at the time. He said I was probably just a bit edgy.

On the penultimate day of The Open, Boxall was paired with Colin Montgomerie. He remembered, 'On the range warming up I couldn't commit to any shot, but I was still able to hit it. I said to Monty round about the first tee that something was wrong with my leg. But he didn't know what was coming up and nor did I. On the eighth both of us hit 1-iron, but I was a long way behind Monty and he asked if there was something wrong. I bogeyed the hole, got to the next tee, took a drink and thought to myself. "I must commit to this next shot". I still didn't know what it was, but it was a bizarre feeling. I hit the 1-iron again and as I did there was this noise like a sack of potatoes splitting and I screamed and collapsed. I'm told the ball flew 240 yards (220 metres) and was right next to Monty's. I was conscious, but didn't know what was going on. Miraculously there was an orthopaedic surgeon watching and he came on the tee. Then an ambulance arrived and took me away.' The official results table showed Boxall finishing 111th and earning £3,000. It would be February 1992 before he was able to return to the golf course

THE ONLY

PLAYER TO ORDER A PIZZA DURING THE US WOMEN'S OPEN

LORI GARBACZ, US WOMEN'S OPEN AT COLONIAL COUNTRY CLUB, 3735 COUNTRY CLUB CIRCLE, FORT WORTH, TEXAS, USA. JULY 1991

Lori Garbacz joined the LPGA Tour in 1979 and five years later came third in the US Women's Open. Talented and attractive, Garbacz does not enjoy the first two rounds of that competition believing that they 'are the slowest a tour pro will ever play'. Garbacz became particularly frustrated at the 1991 Open when she was forced to wait for 45 minutes on the fourth tee. By the time she reached the 14th hole, Garbacz was frustrated and bored, 'so I made a political statement'. Spotting a bank of payphones, she sent her caddie over to order a pizza from Domino's. The caddie told the firm to be at the 17th tee in 45 minutes and sure enough the large cheese pizza and Garbacz arrived at the same time.

THE FIRST

PGA EVENT THAT TIGER WOODS PLAYED IN

NISSAN OPEN, RIVIERA COUNTRY CLUB, 1250 CAPRI DRIVE, PACIFIC PALISADES, CALIFORNIA, USA. SUNDAY 1 MARCH 1992

Eldrick Tont Woods was born at Cypress, California on 30 December 1975 and nicknamed Tiger after Vuong Dang Phong, a Vietnamese friend of his father. Woods began playing golf when he was just two and appeared on *The Mike Douglas Show*. Woods was challenged to a putting contest by fellow guest Bob Hope. When he missed three putts, Woods moaned that the green was not level. He was just three when he shot 48 over nine holes at the Navy Gold Club in Cypress, California. At five, he was given his first complete set of golf clubs and six when he scored his first hole-in-one.

Woods won the World Junior Golf Championship six times, the first when he was just eight. In 1991 he became the youngest Junior Amateur Champion in history aged 15. Sixteen-year-old Tiger Woods appeared in his first PGA event, the Nissan (formerly the Los Angeles) Open as an amateur. It did not take Woods long to get into a winning streak – in 1996 he became the first player to win three consecutive US Amateur championships.

On 27 August 1996 he turned professional and signed contracts to endorse products for Nike and Titleist, reportedly worth $40 million and $20 million respectively. On 15 June 1997 Woods took the number one slot on the official world rankings after just 42 weeks on the PGA Tour. In 2000 he became the youngest player to have won all four Majors – the US Masters in 1997, the US PGA Championship in 1999 and 2000 and the US Open and The Open in 2000.

THE ONLY

PLAYER FINED FOR WEARING SHORTS

Mark Wiebe, Anheuser-Busch Golf Classic, River Course at Kingsmill Golf Club, 1010 Kingsmill Road, Williamsburg, Virginia, USA. July 1992

The US PGA Tour has a strict dress code for players in its tournaments. Golfers are not allowed to wear shorts whatever the weather. Players in the 1992 Anheuser-Busch Golf Classic in Williamsburg found that the day gradually became hotter and hotter till finally the mercury reached 39°C (102°F). Wiebe thought it too hot to wear normal trousers so went out on to the practice tee clad in a pair of shorts. The officials of the PGA did not think heat a reason to break one of their rules so they fined Wiebe $500. He finished in tied 26th position and took home $7,810.

THE FIRST

NATIONAL TOURNAMENT IN

BRITAIN FOR OVER-80S

**LAWRENCE BATLEY OVER-80S CHAMPIONSHIP, MOORTOWN,
HARROGATE ROAD, ALWOODLEY, LEEDS, WEST YORKSHIRE,
ENGLAND. MONDAY 7 SEPTEMBER 1992**

The inaugural Lawrence Batley Over-80s Championship was marred by tragedy. Frank Hart, 83, a member of the Ilkley Club, collapsed by the fourth green and despite the best efforts of medical staff he was pronounced dead on arrival at St James's Hospital in Leeds. The competition was the brainchild of Lawrence Batley, an 82-year-old former tonic wine salesman who made his fortune by pioneering cash-and-carry in the north of England in the 1950s. The oldest of the 93 competitors was George Nunn, aged 90. The tournament used the Stableford scoring system and the winner was Charles Mitchell, 80, who shot one over his age for a score of 39.

THE ONLY

GOLFER TO PLAY THE
SOUTHWESTERN BELL COLONIAL
IN HIS UNDERWEAR

**IAN BAKER-FINCH AT COLONIAL COUNTRY CLUB, 3735 COUNTRY CLUB CIRCLE, FORT WORTH, TEXAS, USA.
SUNDAY 30 MAY 1993**

Two years after he won The Open, Ian Baker-Finch played the Southwestern Bell Colonial, the longest running non-major PGA Tour event to be held at the same site. It has changed its name regularly and since 2007 has been known as Crowne Plaza Invitational at Colonial. On the par 3, 190-yard (173 metres) 13th hole Baker-Finch hit his ball into a water hazard. He doffed his shoes and socks, and then to the shock of spectators, also took off his trousers before wading into the water. Clad below the waist only in his underwear he hit the ball 10 yards (9 metres) past the hole and then missed his putt for a bogey 4. He finished with a score of 277 (74–67–68–68) to finish tied in 33rd position and take home a cheque for $6,034.17.

THE FIRST
ADVERTISING IN COURSE HOLES

ROYAL DORNOCH GOLF CLUB, GOLF ROAD, DORNOCH, SCOTLAND.
FRIDAY 1 OCTOBER 1993

An enterprising advertising salesman found a novel place to promote his client's product – the hole. The product was Glenmorangie Scotch Whisky. However, the members were not happy to have such commercialism on the course and the club did not repeat the exercise when the initial contract expired.

THE FIRST
PRESIDENTS CUP

THE PRESIDENTS CUP AT ROBERT TRENT JONES GOLF CLUB,
1 TURTLE POINT DRIVE, GAINESVILLE, PRINCE WILLIAM COUNTY,
VIRGINIA, USA. FRIDAY 16–SUNDAY 18 SEPTEMBER 1994

The Presidents Cup is a biennial event contested between professional golfers from the United States and the rest of the world, excluding Europe, in non-Ryder Cup years. The idea came from the US PGA and not as some have assumed from President Bill Clinton who was in office at the time of the first competition and a keen amateur golfer. The first Presidents Cup was won by the USA, captained by Hale Irwin, beating the international side led by David Graham, by 20 to 12. The American side retained the trophy in 1996.

THE ONLY

WORLD LEADER TO SCORE 38
UNDER PAR ON HIS FIRST ROUND OF GOLF

KIM JONG-IL, PYONGYANG GOLF CLUB, PYONGYANG, NORTH
KOREA. OCTOBER 1994

The Dear Leader came to power in North Korea on 8 July 1994 on the death of his father Kim Il-Sung, the Great Leader. A true Renaissance man, the diminutive Kim had never played golf until 1994 when he picked up a club at the testing 7,700-yard (7,040 metres) championship course at Pyongyang Golf Club. On the first hole, a 370-yard (338 metres) dogleg par four, Kim hit an eagle two. 'Dear Leader Comrade General Kim Jong-Il, whom I respect from the bottom of my heart, scored two on this hole,' said the course professional Park Young Man. Kim then went on to make five holes-in-one as he shot 34, 38 under par, on the 18 holes. He has been a keen golfer ever since and North Korean state media reports that Kim routinely shoots three or four holes-in-one per round.

THE FIRST

SITTING PRESIDENT TO PLAY
IN A PRO-AM GOLF TOURNAMENT

PRESIDENT WILLIAM JEFFERSON CLINTON, BOB HOPE CHRYSLER
CLASSIC AT BERMUDA DUNES COUNTRY CLUB, 42360 ADAMS STREET,
BERMUDA DUNES, CALIFORNIA, USA. WEDNESDAY 15 FEBRUARY 1995

History was made in 1995 when Bill Clinton became the first sitting president to take part in a pro-am golf tournament. He was part of a team that included Bob Hope, reigning tournament champion Scott Hoch, President George Bush and President Gerald Ford. Some time before the event, President Clinton had stated that it was his ambition to go around a course in fewer than 80 but on the day he came nowhere close.

It did not start off well. President Ford hit his first ball into the crowd while President Clinton sliced his first into a bunker. President Bush's second ball hit old-aged pensioner Norma Earley in the face, breaking her glasses and cutting her nose. Mrs Earley was taken to hospital where her injury required ten stitches. Play continued apace until the 14th hole when President Bush's ball hit another spectator. Fortunately, John Rynd had the good sense to turn his back as the president hit the ball and so it did little damage. President Bush autographed the ball for Mr Rynd as a souvenir.

At the 17th hole President Ford's ball drew blood from spectator Geraldine Grommesh's left index finger when it hit her. By the end of play Hoch had scored 70 (it was a par 68 course) while President Bush scored 92 beating President Clinton by one stroke. He claimed that it was his worst performance in three or four years. President Ford carded 100 but these did not include mulligans (free shots).

THE FIRST
DIVORCÉE TO SUE A GOLF CLUB
OVER MEMBERSHIP
Mary Ann Warfield vs San Mateo Peninsula Golf and Country Club, San Francisco, California, USA. Thursday 29 June 1995

When Mary Ann Warfield was divorced, the judge awarded her husband's golf membership to her as part of the settlement. However, when she went to the San Mateo Peninsula Golf and Country Club they refused her admittance because she was a woman, despite the fact that she was an avid golfer and had won the women's division club championship. Warfield took her case to the San Mateo County Superior Court and then the California Supreme Court which ruled 6–1 in favour of the plaintiff thereby disallowing discrimination based on sex in certain clubs, even those purporting to be private.

Justice Ronald M. George said that the San Mateo club was a business because it had regular business transactions with non-members and therefore could not be construed as completely private. 'Financially, it was devastating. Personally, it was devastating,' said Warfield. 'You go through a divorce, and that is tough enough.'

THE LAST

APPEARANCE OF
ARNOLD PALMER AT THE OPEN

The Open at Old Course at St Andrews, Fife, Scotland.
Sunday 23 July 1995

Arnold Palmer first played at The Open in 1960 and finished second to Kel Nagle of Australia by one stroke. Palmer had asked his long-serving caddie for advice on the 17th hole and James 'Tip' Anderson recommended a 5-iron for the first three rounds. The King disagreed and said that he thought it should be a 6-iron. Finally, on each of the three rounds Palmer took his caddie's advice and each time he bungled the hole. On the fourth round, Palmer ignored his caddie and used the 6-iron only for the ball to overshoot the green and end up on the road as had so many other balls before and since.

Palmer managed to recover and made his only par of the competition. 'There you are, Tip,' said Palmer, 'You've been giving me the wrong club all week and it's cost us the championship.' The following year in 1961 Palmer won the competition to triumph in his fourth Major. The next year, he returned to Britain and retained his Open title. In 1995 Palmer returned to say farewell to Britain at his favourite course of St Andrews. He missed the cut as he had done the previous occasion he played The Open in 1990. That year Palmer, Anderson and a group of friends went on a tour of Fife's bars. Anderson was in tears, 'I should have done better,' he wailed. Palmer grasped his hand, 'No, we should have done better, old friend.'

THE ONLY

PLAYER TO WIN
PGA PLAYER OF THE YEAR IN HIS SECOND SEASON

TIGER WOODS. 1997

In 1996 *Sports Illustrated* named Tiger Woods as its Sportsman of the Year. He was also named PGA Rookie of the Year by the PGA Tour. The following year he became the first and to date only golfer named as PGA Player of the Year in his second season in the game.

THE ONLY
PLAYER TO WITHDRAW FROM THE US OPEN
AFTER BREAKING HIS HAND
IN A HOTEL

JOSÉ MARIA OLAZÁBAL, US OPEN AT COURSE NUMBER 2, PINEHURST RESORT, 80 CAROLINA VISTA DRIVE, VILLAGE OF PINEHURST, NORTH CAROLINA,USA. JUNE 1999

In June 1999 Spaniard José Maria Olazábal withdrew from the US Open after a poor first round showing. Returning to his hotel room, he was so annoyed with himself that he punched the wall of his room. As he did so, he broke a bone in his hand and had to pull out of the tournament.

THE ONLY
DOUBLE US OPEN CHAMPION
KILLED IN AN
AEROPLANE CRASH

PAYNE STEWART, EDMONDS COUNTY, MINA, SOUTH DAKOTA, USA. MONDAY 25 OCTOBER 1999

William Payne Stewart joined the PGA Tour in 1982. He won the 1989 PGA Championship and the US Open 1991 and 1999 becoming the last player, to date, over 40 to win the championship. On five occasions he represented the United States in the Ryder Cup (1987 at Muirfield Village Golf Club, Dublin, Ohio; 1989 on the Brabazon Course at the Belfry, Sutton Coldfield; 1991 at the Ocean Course, Kiawah Island Golf Resort, South Carolina; 1993 on the Brabazon Course at the Belfry, Sutton Coldfield; 1999 at the Country Club, Brookline, Massachusetts).

A month after the Ryder Cup, Stewart and three other passengers: golf course designer Bruce Borland, and two of Stewart's agents – Van Ardan and Robert Fraley, the president and CEO of Leader Enterprises, along with two pilots (former US Air Force Captain Michael Kling and Flight Officer Stephanie Bellegarrigue) boarded a chartered Learjet 35 to fly between Orlando, Florida, and Dallas, Texas. The plane took off at 1.09 pm. Fourteen minutes into the flight there was no response from the cockpit so a US Air Force F-16 fighter from the 40th Flight Test Squadron at Eglin Air Force Base at Orlando, Florida, was sent to investigate. At an altitude of 46,400 ft (14,000 metres) the fighter pilot radioed the Learjet but received no reply. The pilot said that he could see no movement in the cockpit. He returned to base. Three hours later, another two F-16s reported the same as did a third fighter. At 5.13 pm the plane crashed at Edmonds County, Mina, South Dakota. There were no survivors.

It appeared that all the passengers and crew had died of hypoxia (lack of oxygen) due to decompression in the aircraft cabin and cockpit. In 2000 Stewart's widow, Tracey, and Mr Fraley's family brought a lawsuit against the Learjet's operator SunJet Aviation Inc and owner JetShares One Inc demanding an over-the-top $200 million. The suit was dismissed. In 2001, Stewart was posthumously inducted into the World Golf Hall of Fame.

THE ONLY

WOMAN TO BREAK 60

ANNIKA SÖRENSTAM, STANDARD REGISTER PING, MOON VALLEY COUNTRY CLUB, 151 WEST MOON VALLEY DRIVE, PHOENIX, ARIZONA, USA. FRIDAY 16 MARCH 2001

Annika Sörenstam was born at Bro, near Stockholm in Sweden on 9 October 1970. Her younger sister Charlotta also plays golf and they are the only sisters to have both won $1 million on the LPGA circuit.

In the spring of 2001 she became the first and to date only woman to go around in fewer than 60 strokes in a professional competition when she achieved the feat at the Standard Register Ping tournament. She shot 31 on the first nine holes and just 28 on the back nine. The round included 13 birdies, no bogeys and just 25 putts on the 6,459-yard (5900 metres) course. Sörenstam missed just one fairway, reached every green in regulation, and her longest par putt was 3½ feet. She said, 'I made such an incredible start, and it was such fun, to put it mildly. By the end, I started to get very nervous. But now I'm so proud and happy.'

Ironically, Charlotta Sörenstam was the tournament's defending champion. Two years later, Annika Sörenstam became the first woman since 1945 to play in a men's PGA Tour event when she played at the Bank of America Colonial tournament.

THE FIRST

PLAYER TO HOLD ALL FOUR MAJOR TITLES AT SAME TIME

TIGER WOODS, US OPEN AT PEBBLE BEACH GOLF LINKS, 1700 17 MILE DRIVE, PEBBLE BEACH, CALIFORNIA, USA. SUNDAY 18 JUNE 2000; THE OPEN AT OLD COURSE AT ST ANDREWS, FIFE, SCOTLAND. SATURDAY 22 JULY 2000; US PGA CHAMPIONSHIP AT VALHALLA GOLF CLUB, 15503 SHELBYVILLE ROAD, LOUISVILLE, KENTUCKY, USA. SUNDAY 20 AUGUST 2000; US MASTERS AT AUGUSTA NATIONAL GOLF CLUB, 2604 WASHINGTON ROAD, AUGUSTA, GEORGIA, USA. SUNDAY 4 APRIL 2001

In June 2000 Tiger Woods hit a record equalling 272 (65–69–71–67) to win the US Open at Pebble Beach and $800,000. He finished 15 strokes ahead of Ernie Els and Miguel Angel Jimenez. Woods's opening round of 65 was the lowest for the US Open at Pebble Beach and he sank a one putt on 34 holes and made two putts on all the rest. The following month, he flew to Scotland where he won The Open on the Old Course at St Andrews. He scored 269 (67–66–67–69) to finish 19 under par, which put him eight strokes head of Ernie Els. In August 2000 Woods was lucky to win the US PGA Championship, having tied with Bob May on 270 (66–67–70–67), 18 under par, before winning the play-off by one shot over three holes. Woods equalled Ben Hogan's record of three Majors in one season. Eight months later, Woods added the US Masters title to his list of tournament triumphs when he beat David Duval by two shots. However, Wood's triumph did not count as a Grand Slam because he did not win them in the same calendar year.

THE FIRST
DISABLED GOLFER
TO SUE US PGA
OVER GOLF CART USE

PGA Tour, Inc vs Martin, Supreme Court of the USA, Washington DC, USA. Tuesday 29 May 2001

Casey Martin was born at Eugene, Oregon on 2 June 1972 with a disability in his right leg known as Klippel Trenaunay Weber syndrome, a circulatory problem that makes walking difficult. The lower leg atrophies and the tibia can become so brittle that it has to be amputated. He turned professional in 1995 but because of the pain in his leg needed to use a golf cart, which was banned under PGA rules. He sued the US PGA Tour over the right to use a cart under the Americans with Disabilities Act and as the case wound its way through the courts he did indeed use a cart.

In 1998 he won the Lakeland Classic, which meant that he had a five-year exemption from Qualifying School where golfers who finish below a certain level have to go to gain a place on the PGA Tour and the Nike Tour (later the Buy.com Tour, and now the Nationwide Tour), the second tier competition. In 1999 Martin finished 14th on the Nike Tour money list to win himself a place on the PGA Tour. However, he finished 179th on the money list in 2000 and lost his spot.

On 17 January 2001 his case was heard before the Supreme Court of the USA. On 29 May 2001 the court ruled 7–2 in Martin's favour. Justice John Paul Stevens said, '[This decision will] allow Martin the chance to qualify for and compete in the athletic events [the PGA Tour] offers to those members of the public who have the skill and desire to enter. That is exactly what the [Americans With Disabilities Act] requires. I think in the future this opens some doors for people. An institution like the PGA Tour ... before they just automatically knock down someone's desire for accommodation, they might have to think twice.' Martin said, 'I'm thrilled, overjoyed. It's been 3½ years of waiting, and I finally got the answer that I really wanted. At least I don't have to worry about the cart being taken away from me. It's mine for good now.'

THE ONLY
PLAYER TO WIN THREE
WOMEN'S BRITISH OPEN
CHAMPIONSHIPS

KARRIE WEBB. WOMEN'S BRITISH OPEN CHAMPIONSHIP AT WOBURN GOLF AND COUNTRY CLUB, LITTLE BRICKHILL, MILTON KEYNES, ENGLAND. 1995; SUNNINGDALE GOLF CLUB, RIDGEMOUNT ROAD, ASCOT, ENGLAND. 1997; AILSA COURSE AT TURNBERRY, MAIDENS ROAD, AYRSHIRE, SCOTLAND. 2002

Born at Ayr, Queensland, Australia on 21 December 1974, Karrie Webb turned professional in 1994 and the following year – her first full year as a professional – became the youngest winner of the Women's British Open, going round the course at Woburn in 278 strokes and winning by seven shots, going 14 under par. Two years later, she won the title again, improving on her score by hitting 269 and going 19 under par. She became the only three-time winner in 2002 when she went round in 273. In 2005 she became the youngest living person inducted into the World Golf Hall of Fame.

THE FIRST
CANADIAN TO WIN A MAJOR TOURNAMENT

MIKE WEIR, US MASTERS AT AUGUSTA NATIONAL GOLF CLUB, 2604 WASHINGTON ROAD, AUGUSTA, GEORGIA, USA. SUNDAY 13 APRIL 2003

Mike Weir, at 32, became the first Canadian to win a Major, and the first left-handed golfer to win the US Masters when he beat Len Mattiace on the first play-off hole. In 2003 Weir also became the first left-hander to win the Nissan (Los Angeles) Open.

THE LAST
PLAYER TO DATE TO WIN THE OPEN AT FIRST ATTEMPT

Ben Curtis, The Open at the Royal St George's Golf Club, Sandwich, Kent, England. Sunday 20 July 2003

The first winner of The Open at the first attempt was obviously the first winner (Willie Park in 1860) but in the 150 or so years since, only nine players have emulated that feat. On one occasion debutants have won at the first attempt in consecutive years – on 4 October 1873 Tom Kidd won at St Andrews (by one stroke) and the following year on 10 April 1874 Mungo Park won at Musselburgh (by two strokes). The most recent debut winner of the Claret Jug was Ben Curtis in 2003. He beat Thomas Bjorn and Vijay Singh by one stroke – 283 to 284 to win the Claret Jug and £700,000.

THE FIRST

PLAYER TO APPEAR AT THE US MASTERS 50 CONSECUTIVE TIMES

ARNOLD PALMER, US MASTERS AT AUGUSTA NATIONAL GOLF CLUB, 2604 WASHINGTON ROAD, AUGUSTA, GEORGIA, USA. THURSDAY 8 APRIL 2004

At the 2004 Masters Arnold Palmer, four times winner of the green jacket, became the first player to have appeared 50 consecutive times at Augusta. In 2007 Gary Player, then 71, became the second player to achieve the feat.

THE ONLY

WAG CONVICTED OF MONEY LAUNDERING

SHERRIE DALY, LEXINGTON, KENTUCKY, USA. FRIDAY 12 NOVEMBER 2004

On 29 July 2001 John Daly married Sherrie Miller, his fourth wife, seven weeks after meeting her at the FedEx St Jude Classic in Memphis, Tennessee. In that year he finished 61st in the Money List with $830,000. Two years later, things had gone downhill for Mr and Mrs Daly. He was disqualified or failed to make the cut in 16 out of 22 tournaments he entered, and went into rehab again to try and battle his problems with drink. On 28 July 2003, five days after John Daly Jr. was born, Sherrie Daly was indicted in Mississippi, along with her parents Alvis and Billie Miller, for their participation in what authorities said was a drug ring and an illegal gambling operation.

According to court documents, Alvis Miller conspired to conduct financial transactions through the acquisition and distribution of crystal methamphetamine, cocaine and marijuana, illegal gambling operations and the concealment and disguising of the source of ownership of proceeds in excess of $1.2 million. On 12 November 2004 Sherrie Daly admitted her guilt to a charge of conspiracy to structure a transaction to evade the reporting requirement in a plea bargain. On 26 January 2006, she reported to prison in Lexington, Kentucky, where she served five months and then served five months of house arrest on her release. The couple has since divorced.

THE FIRST
PLAYER TO EARN $10 MILLION IN A SEASON
VIJAY SINGH. 2004

Born at Lautoka, Fiji on 22 February 1963, Vijay Singh began his record-breaking year by winning the AT&T Pebble Beach National Pro-Am and collecting $954,000 in prize money. He won the US PGA Championship in a three-hole play-off over Justin Leonard and Chris DiMarco. On 6 September 2004 Singh won the Deutsche Bank Championship in Norton, Massachusetts and took over the number one spot in the Official World Golf Rankings from Tiger Woods after Woods had spent 264 weeks at the top. Singh finished the 2004 season with a career best nine victories and $10,905,166 in earnings. Unsurprisingly, he was named the PGA Tour's and PGA of America's Player of the Year.

THE FIRST
WOMEN'S WORLD CUP
THE WORLD CUP AT FANCOURT GOLF COURSE, MONTAGU STREET, BLANCO, GEORGE, SOUTH AFRICA. FRIDAY 11–SUNDAY 13 FEBRUARY 2005

Almost 52 years after the men's World Cup began the women got in on the act in post-apartheid South Africa. Practice rounds were held on

7–9 February and the opening ceremony took place at the Fancourt Conference Hall on 10 February. The main event attracted around 1,400 visitors and guests on the first day, and 4,100 on the next. The first winners of the three-day event of 18 holes of foursomes, a round of better ball and strokeplay were Rui Kitada and Ai Muyazato of Japan.

THE ONLY
PLAYER TO APPEAR ON BANKNOTES
JACK NICKLAUS. THURSDAY 14 JULY 2005

Jack Nicklaus, claimed by many to be the greatest golfer of all time, has received many accolades. In 1974 he was inducted into the World Golf Hall of Fame. Twenty-one years later, he became the only living person to have appeared on a Scottish bank note apart from Elizabeth II and the Queen Mother. On the first day of The Open the Royal Bank of Scotland issued two million Nicklaus commemorative £5 notes. Nicklaus said:

'I think that the honour that RBS has given me with the £5 note is unbelievable. It is something that I have a hard time describing. When RBS approached me and said, "Jack, we'd like to put you on the £5 note," obviously I said I'm deeply honoured. It's one of the most memorable honours that I've had in my career.'

THE LAST
MAJOR TOURNAMENT
PLAYED BY JACK NICKLAUS
THE OPEN AT OLD COURSE AT ST ANDREWS, FIFE, SCOTLAND. FRIDAY 15 JULY 2005

Tragedy touched the life of the Golden Bear on 1 March 2005 when his 17-month-old grandson (the son of second son Steve Nicklaus) drowned in a tragic accident. A month later, Nicklaus played in the US Masters at the suggestion of Steve in a bid to come to terms with their joint grief. That summer Nicklaus played his last Major tournament before retirement and Steve Nicklaus acted as his father's caddie. In his final round Nicklaus played with Luke Donald and Tom Watson. When he had played his second round tee shot on the 18th hole, the crowd gave Nicklaus a ten-minute standing ovation. His last shot was sinking a 5 yard (4.5 metre) birdie putt. He scored 72 but missed the 36-hole cut by three shots.

THE FIRST
LEXUS CUP

**TANAH MERAH COUNTRY CLUB, 25 CHANGI COAST ROAD
(S)499803, SINGAPORE. FRIDAY 9–SUNDAY 11 DECEMBER 2005**

With the rise in popularity of golf in the Far East more competitions are being held there. The Lexus Cup for professional lady golfers lasted only until 2008 and saw a team from Asia taking on one from the rest of the world. For the first competition there was a purse of $960,000 ($50,000 to each member of the winning team and $30,000 each to the losing team). The captain of the Asia team was Grace Park while Annika Sörenstam led the rest of the world in all four tournaments.

The Lexus Cup was contested over three days with every golfer playing on each day. On the first day there were six foursomes matches. The second day had six four-balls and the final day 12 singles matches, with a play-off between the captains if the scores were tied at the end of the singles matches. The first was won by the rest of the world after which Sörenstam said optimistically but not as it turned out accurately, 'I think it is a great tournament that will continue to grow.' The second Lexus Cup, also held at the Tanah Merah Country Club, from 15–17 December 2006 saw Asia win by 12½ to 11½. The third (at the Vines Golf and Country Club, Perth, Australia on 7–9 December 2007) was a more convincing victory for Asia under the captaincy of Se Ri Pak at 15–9. The final Lexus Cup was held at Singapore Island Country Club, Singapore on 28–30 November 2008 and was won by the rest of the world by 12½ to 11½.

THE FIRST

ROYAL TROPHY

AMATA SPRING COUNTRY CLUB, CHONBURI, BANGKOK, THAILAND.
THURSDAY 5–SUNDAY 8 JANUARY 2006

A new tournament for professional men's teams golf began in the Far East at the start of 2006. Like the Ryder Cup, the Royal Trophy uses three different formats – foursomes (alternate shot) on the opening day followed by four-ball on day two and singles on the last day.

The eight-man teams are from Asia and Europe and were captained respectively by Japan's Masahiro Kuramoto and Severiano Ballesteros from Spain. The Asian team consisted of two Thais, two Indians, two Japanese, a Chinese and a Korean. Apart from Ballesteros, Europe's team was made up of David Howell, Paul McGinley, Thomas Bjorn, Kenneth Ferrie, Henrik Stenson, Graeme McDowell, Ian Woosnam and Nick Faldo.

Europe won the first trophy by 9–7 although at one stage they had a 6–2 lead and looked to overwhelm their opponents. Kuramoto commented, 'For a moment it looked possible that we could upset Europe as our players grew in confidence. I was happy to see the boys fight back.' The 2008 event was cancelled because of the death of the King of Thailand's sister. The tournament will be held in Thailand until 2011 when it will be staged in Europe and Asia in alternate years.

THE FIRST

WOMAN INVITED TO PLAY
ON MEN'S EUROPEAN TOUR

MICHELLE WIE, MONDAY 15 MAY 2006

Born at Honolulu, Hawaii on 11 October 1989, the daughter of South Korea's women's amateur golf champion, Michelle Wie began playing golf when she was just four, and six years later she became the youngest player to qualify for the Women's US Amateur Public Links Championship. The record was finally broken by Allisen Corpuz, five months younger than Wie at the time, who was also coincidentally from Hawaii.

In 2002 Wie won the Hawaii State Open Women's Division with a winning margin of 13 shots. In June of the following year she triumphed in the Women's Amateur Public Links tournament making her the youngest winner of a USGA adult event. On 5 October 2005 Wie turned professional and played her first pro tournament, the LPGA Samsung World Championship, where she was disqualified for signing an incorrect scorecard.

On 15 May 2006 Wie played a round of par 72 at Turtle Bay Resort, Oahu to pass the qualification stakes for the US Open. In fact, her score was better than any of the other 40 players. However, she did not go on to win the men's title.

In September 2006 she played in the Omega European Masters but finished last of the 156 players, missing the cut by 14 strokes. By 31 December 2006 she had taken part in 12 men's competitions and failed to make the cut in 11 of them.

THE LAST

GOLF CLUB TO GAIN A 'ROYAL TITLE'

THE ROYAL MAYFAIR GOLF AND COUNTRY CLUB, SOUTH GROAT ROAD, EDMONTON, ALBERTA, CANADA. JULY 2006

Since the Perth Club became the first golf club with the right to include 'Royal' in its name in 1833, more than 60 clubs have the right to call themselves Royal. The last to date is the Royal Mayfair, which was designed by legendary Canadian golf-course designer Stanley Thompson.

THE FIRST
PRAYER MEETING HELD ON US PGA CHAMPIONSHIP COURSE
Medinah Country Club, 6N001 Medinah Road, Medinah, Illinois, USA. Thursday 17 August 2006

Just before the start of the 2006 US PGA Championship at Medinah Country Club (the second time the championship had been held there, the first being in 1999), Tom Lehman, the captain of that year's American Ryder Cup team, held a prayer meeting on the side of the 18th green. The prayers coincided with the funeral of Heather Clarke, the wife of golfer Darren, who died from breast cancer on 13 August 2006.

THE FIRST
RYDER CUP MATCH WON BY A HOLE-IN-ONE
PAUL CASEY AND DAVID HOWELL VS STEWART CINK AND ZACH JOHNSON. RYDER CUP AT THE K CLUB, STRAFFAN, COUNTY KILDARE, IRELAND. SATURDAY 23 SEPTEMBER 2006

In their foursomes match Paul Casey and David Howell faced Americans Stewart Cink and Zach Johnson and were leading 4 and 5 as they approached the par-three, 213-yard (195 metres) 14th hole. Casey selected a four-iron and teed up his ball. He struck it and to the amazement of himself, not to mention the spectators watching, the ball sailed into the air and then landed on the green and settled in the cup to give him and Howell a 5 and 4 win. Casey's hole-in-one was the first Ryder Cup hole-in-one since 1995 when Howard Clark sank one at Oak Hill.

To add to the general delight, Europe won the 2006 Ryder Cup by exactly the margin of 2004, 18½ points to 9½. Casey's shot was named by the Royal Bank of Scotland as its shot of 2006. Ladbrokes bookmakers revealed that more than £8 million was gambled on the first day of the 2006 Ryder Cup, setting a record.

THE LAST

TOURNAMENT MATCH
PLAYED BY ARNOLD PALMER

**CHAMPIONS TOUR'S ADMINISTAFF SMALL BUSINESS CLASSIC
AT AUGUSTA PINES GOLF CLUB, 18 AUGUSTA PINES DRIVE,
SPRING, TEXAS, USA. FRIDAY 13 OCTOBER 2006**

In 2004, Arnold Palmer competed in the US Masters for the 50th and last time. Since 2007 he has been the honorary starter for the tournament. Palmer's last tournament game was on an autumnal day in 2006. Playing in the Champions Tour's Administaff Small Business Classic, Palmer became increasingly unhappy with his performance and gave up after just four holes. He played the rest of the greens but did not keep a score card.

THE FIRST

GOLFING RECIPIENT OF A
CONGRESSIONAL
GOLD MEDAL

BYRON NELSON. WASHINGTON DC, USA. MONDAY 16 OCTOBER 2006

Following his death on 26 September 2006 a number of posthumous honours were awarded to Byron Nelson. The names of a number of roads were changed either to his name or associations thereof. On 16 October 2006 President George W. Bush awarded Nelson the medal under P.L. 109–357, 120 Stat. 2044–2046: 'To award a Congressional gold medal to Byron Nelson in recognition of his significant contributions to the game of golf as a player, a teacher, and a commentator'. All Congressional Gold Medal legislation must be co-sponsored by at least two-thirds (290) of the Members of the House of Representatives and at least 67 senators must co-sponsor any Congressional Gold Medal legislation before the committee will consider it.

Other winners include: George Washington (1776), Wright brothers (1909), Charles Lindbergh (1928), Howard Hughes (1939), Irving Berlin (1954), Bob Hope (1962), Walt Disney (1968), Senator Robert F. Kennedy (1978), John Wayne (1979, his 70th birthday and 16 days before his death), Frank Sinatra (1997), Pope John Paul II (2000), President and Nancy Reagan (2000) and Tony Blair (2003). On 30 September 2009 Arnold Palmer became the second golfer to be honoured.

THE FIRST

ARGENTINEAN
TO WIN THE US OPEN

ANGEL CABRERA, US OPEN AT OAKMONT COUNTRY CLUB, 1233 HULTON ROAD, OAKMONT, PENNSYLVANIA, USA. SUNDAY 17 JUNE 2007

In 2007 Argentinean Angel Cabrera became the first Argentinean and last foreigner (to date) to win the US Open. He had begun caddying when he was ten and a benefactor bought him his first set of clubs when he was 16. Until he gave up, he chain-smoked at every links where he played. He turned professional in 1989, winning his first tournaments (Paraguay Open and El Rodeo Open in Colombia) in 1995.

Twelve years later, he won the 107th US Open, beating Tiger Woods and Jim Furyk by one stroke and taking home a cheque for $1.26 million. At the end of the first round, he lay in second place with 68, one stroke behind Briton Nick Dougherty. By the end of the second round, Cabrera was in the lead with a par score of 140, one ahead of Bubba Watson. The third round was potentially disastrous for Cabrera as he finished tied in seventh place with a score of 216, four behind the Australian leader Aaron Baddeley with Tiger Woods in second place. On the last day, Cabrera scored a birdie at one of the longest par-3 holes in Major history when he sunk a 7 yard (6.5 metres) putt at the eighth hole. He finished scoring 69 for the round to give him the title. At a post-match interview Cabrera said, 'Well, there are some players that have psychologists, some have sportologists, I smoke.

THIS PLAYER IS ALSO WELL-KNOWN AS: The LAST non-American winner, to date, of the US Open

THE FIRST
BANNING OF MOBILES
AT THE OPEN

The Open at Carnoustie Golf Club, 3 Links Parade, Carnoustie, Angus, Scotland. Sunday 22 July 2007

In 2006 contestants playing in The Open at Hoylake moaned to the organizing committee that the constant ringing of mobiles was off-putting as they tried to play a shot. On 22 January 2007 the Royal & Ancient Club announced a ban on mobiles at Carnoustie that summer for The Open. Mobiles were also forbidden at the other three Majors and the Ryder Cup.

THE ONLY
US PRESIDENT
INDUCTED INTO THE
GOLF WORLD HALL OF FAME

DWIGHT D. EISENHOWER. 2009

The 34th president of the United States and a five-star general, Dwight David Eisenhower (1890–1969) began playing golf in his mid-thirties and played off an 18 handicap. President from 1953 until 20 January 1961, he had a putting green installed on the White House lawn and would on occasion leave the Oval Office for a round. During his time at 1600 Pennsylvania Avenue, he made 29 trips to Augusta where he often played a round with Arnold Palmer.

When Eisenhower was asked how his game had changed since leaving the White House, he replied, 'A lot more people beat me now.' Such was Eisenhower's association with the sport that when the libidinous John F. Kennedy was elected president in November 1960, it was said that one of his staffers said, 'This administration is going to do for sex what the last one did for golf.'

THE FIRST
WOMAN EXPOSED AS A MISTRESS OF TIGER WOODS

Jaimee Grubbs. USA. November 2009

For years Tiger Woods projected an image of devoted family man that enabled him to bank millions of dollars from advertising and product endorsement. His marriage to Elin Nordegren, the mother of his two children, Sam and Charlie, seemed stable and happy. On 15 November 2009 Woods won the Australian Open. Twelve days later, a news story broke that Woods had been involved in a car accident outside his home late at night.

After that at least a dozen women came forward – including two porn stars, Holly Sampson and Joslyn James – claiming to be lovers of Woods. The first was a cocktail waitress with the unfortunate name of Jaimee Grubbs. She claimed that they had met in June 2007 and begun a fling that lasted 31 months. In December 2009 Woods announced that he would not be playing a round (of golf, that is) until 2012.

However, on 19 February 2010 he made his first public appearance at a carefully staged press conference at the Sawgrass Golf Club in Florida, the home of the PGA Tour. Woods spoke for 15 minutes and expressed his regret at his behaviour. A fleet of camera trucks descended on the club. However, only one camera was allowed inside and only journalists from Associated Press, Reuters and Bloomberg were invited to attend. The Golf Writers Association of America boycotted the event after being told they could not ask any questions. It also annoyed fellow golfers who were participating in the Accenture Match Play Championship in Arizona.

Accenture was the first sponsor to drop Woods after the scandal. Ernie Els said, 'It is selfish, and you can write that. I feel sorry for the sponsors. Mondays are a good day to make statements, not Fridays. This takes a lot away from the golf tournament.' Wood said, 'I thought I could get away with it. I thought I was entitled thanks to money and fame, I was wrong.' In March 2010 Woods announced that he would return at the US Masters on 8 April 2010.

BIBLIOGRAPHY

Books

Alliss, Peter *The Who's Who of Golf* (London: Orbis, *1983*)

– with Rab MacWilliam *Alliss' 19th Hole* (London: Arcane, *2005*)

Bartlett, Donald L. and James B. Steele *Howard Hughes His Life and Madness* (London: Andre Deutsch, *2003*)

Bathroom Readers' Institute *Uncle John's Bathroom Reader Tees off on Golf* (Ashland, Bathroom Readers' Press, *2005*)

Beadle, Jeremy *Jeremy Beadle's Today's the Day* (London: W.H. Allen, *1979*)

– *Today's the Day* (New York: Signet, *1981*)

Carpozi, Jr, George *The Fabulous Life of Bing Crosby* (New York: Manor Books, *1977*)

Carruth, Gorton & Eugene Ehrlich *Facts & Dates of American Sports* (New York: Harper & Row, *1988*)

Conner, Floyd *Golf's Most Wanted: The Top 10 Book Of Golf's Outrageous Duffers, Deadly Divots, And Other Oddities* (Washington DC: Brassey's, *2001*)

Franck, Irene M. and David M. Brownstone *Famous First Facts about Sports* (New York: H.W. Wilson, *2001*)

Fraser, Lady Antonia *Mary, Queen of Scots* (London: Granada, *1981*)

Guy, John *My Heart Is My Own: A Life of Mary, Queen of Scots* (London: Fourth Estate, *2004*)

Harris, Ed *Golf Facts, Figures & Fun* (Wisley: Facts, Figures & Fun, *2007*)

Hildreth, Peter *Name-Dropper: Profiles of the Top Names of our Times* (London: McWhirter Publishing, *1970*)

Kane, Joseph Nathan, Steven Anzovin & Janet Podell *Famous First Facts* (6th Ed) (New York: H.W. Wilson, *2006*)

Martin, Chris *The Golfer's Companion* (London: Robson Books, *2005*)

Matthew, H.C.G. and Sir Brian Harrison (Eds) *Oxford Dictionary of National Biography* (Oxford: Oxford University Press, *2004*)

McWhirter, Norris (Ed.) *The Guinness Book of Records 1984* (Enfield: Guinness Superlatives, *1983*)

Moore, Edwin *Scotland 1,000 Things you need to Know* (London: Atlantic Books, *2008*)

Mortimer, David *Classic Golf Clangers* (London: Robson Books, *2005*)

Mosley, Charles (Ed.) *Burke's Peerage, Baronetage & Knightage (107th Ed)* (Wilmington: Burke's Peerage, *2003*)

Sounes, Howard *The Wicked Game: Arnold Palmer, Jack Nicklaus, Tiger Woods and the True Story Of Modern Golf* (London: Sidgwick & Jackson, *2004*)

Steel, Donald *The Guinness Book of Golf Facts and Feats* (2nd Ed) (Enfield: Guinness Superlatives, *1982*)

Wallechinsky, David *The Complete Book of the Olympics* (London: Aurum Press, *2004*)

Ward, Andrew *Golf's Strangest Rounds* (London: Robson Books, *2007*)

Weir, Alison *Mary, Queen of Scots and the Murder of Lord Darnley* (New York: Ballantine Books, *2003*)

Wexler, Daniel *The Book of Golfers* (Ann Arbor: Sports Media Group, *2005*)

White, John *The Golf Miscellany* (London: Carlton Books, *2007*)

Winn, Christopher *I Never Knew that about Scotland* (London: Ebury Press, *2007*)

– *I Never Knew that about The Scottish* (London: Ebury Press, *2009*)

Newspapers

The Independent

New York Times.

Websites

www.attpbgolf.com
bbc.co.uk
champexhibit.pgalinks.com
www.cricketarchive.com
www.curtiscup.org
www.dumfriesmuseum.demon.co.uk
en.wikipedia.org
www.europeantour.com
www.financialexpress.com
www.glenviewclub.com
www.golfeurope.com
www.golflink.com
www.golfpiste.fi
www.golfstats.com
www.golftoday.co.uk
www.golf-information.info
www.hersheycountryclub.com
www.hickorygolfers.com
www.imdb.com
www.johndaly.com
www.masters.com
www.medinahcc.org

www.musselburgholdlinks.co.uk
www.nicklaus.com
www.ohiohistorycentral.org
www.opengolf.com
www.paugolfclub.com
www.pgamediaguide.com
www.randa.org
www.royaladelaidegolf.com.au
www.theroyalandancientgolfclub.org
www.royalbirkdale.com
www.royaldornoch.com
www.royal-perth-golfing-society.org.uk
www.royalstgeorges.com
www.sandagolfclub.co.uk
www.standrews.org.uk
www.struckbylightning.org
www.thecanadianencyclopedia.com
www.royalcinqueports.com
www.theroyaltrophy.com
www.usga.org
www.usopen.com
www.uswamateur.org
www.uswomensopen.com
www.wentworthclub.com
www.wghof.com
www.wgv.com

Executive Editor - Trevor Davies
Senior Editor – Lisa John
Deputy Creative Director - Karen Sawyer
Designer - Janis Utton
Production Manager - David Hearn